MOSAIC ANIMAL
COLORING BOOK

MOSAIC ANIMAL COLORING BOOK

Tips for using this book

Designs begin easy and get harder towards the end of the book (More, smaller sections to color in)

We suggest using fine pens or pencils that will not bleed (leak) too much.

Although designs are not back to back, we recommend placing a scrap piece of paper under the design you are coloring in to avoid bleed.

Do not be afraid to go over (some) lines. Many sections are tiny - it is up to you to choose which contour lines to stay within, and which to combine to choose your own patterns. Not only does it encourage creative thinking, it also helps to make each individual work differently to the last.

Embrace the weirdness! You may see that the animals are missing an eye or have a strange shaped foot. Embrace it! This animals are not drawn 100% anatomically correct.

Be colorful! No one wants to see another black and white killer whale or grey koala. Pick some colors - as many as you want, and start coloring in. The more colorful the better!

Have fun and take your time! Coloring in should not be a chore - you should not force yourself to finish a page when you do not feel like it, and you should not rush to finish any piece of art! Slow down and enjoy the process

Backgrounds are left blank - but feel free to add your own. You may choose to continue with the mosaic theme, or create something special of your own!

© Zoe Tealswan

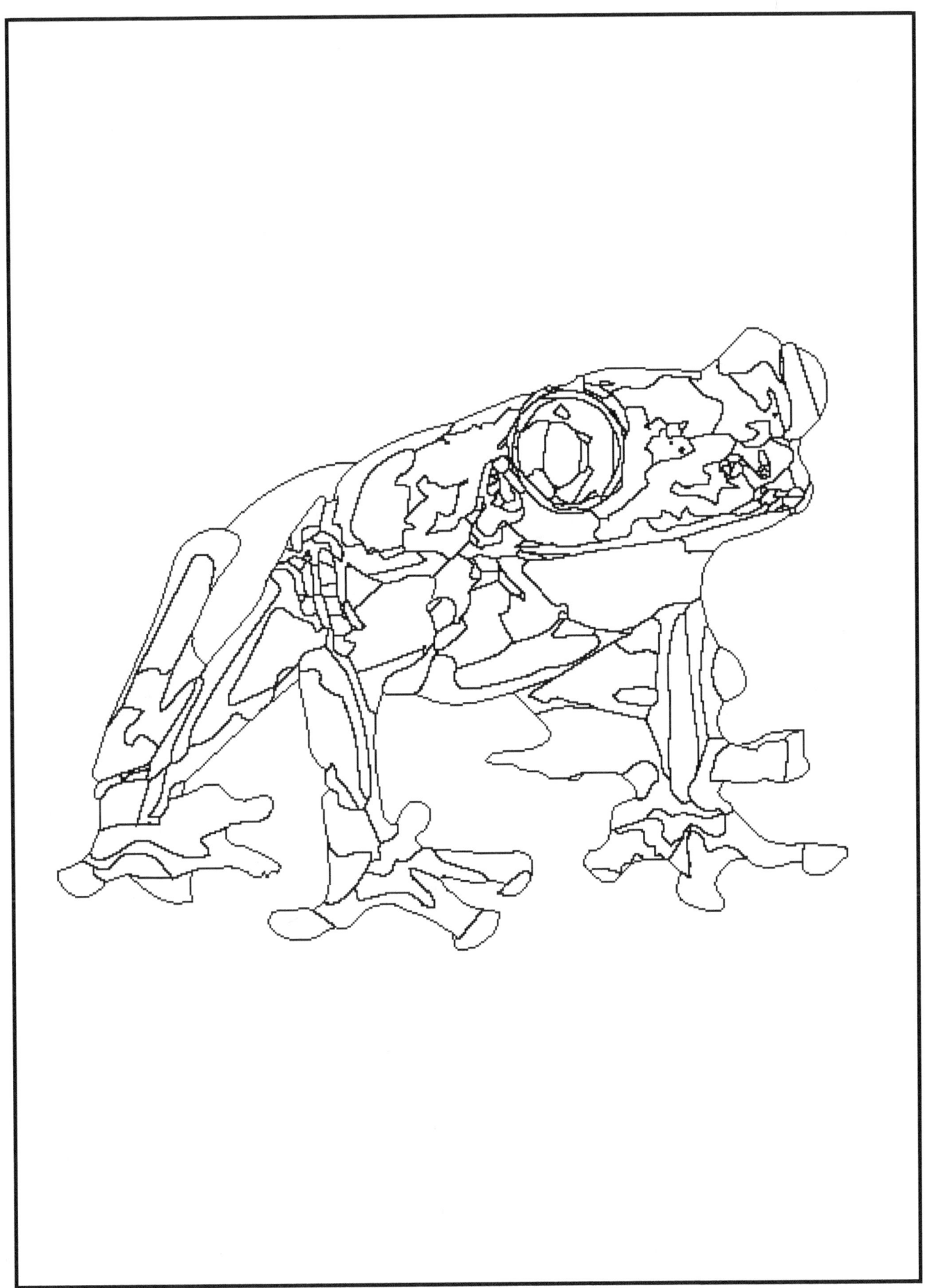

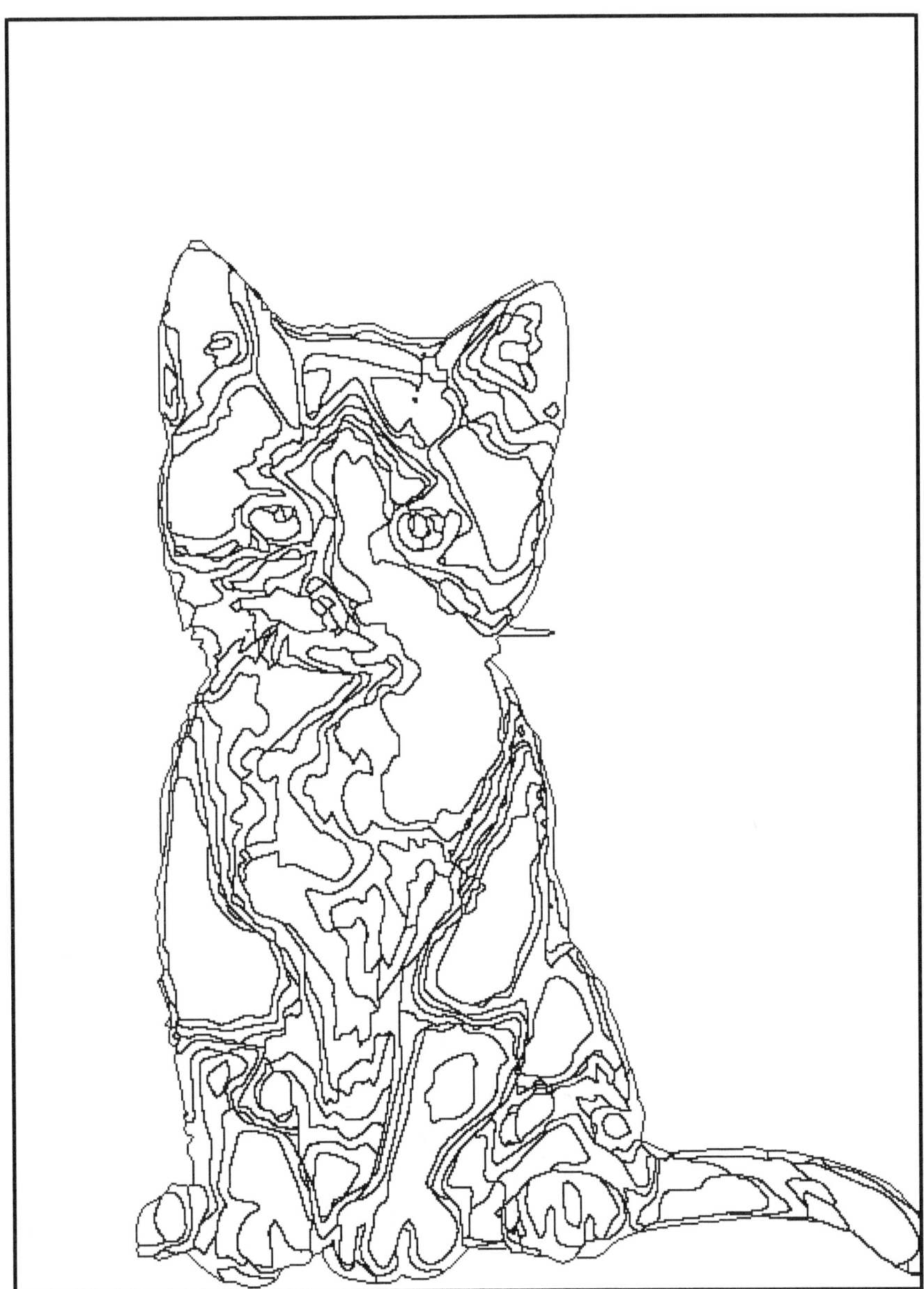

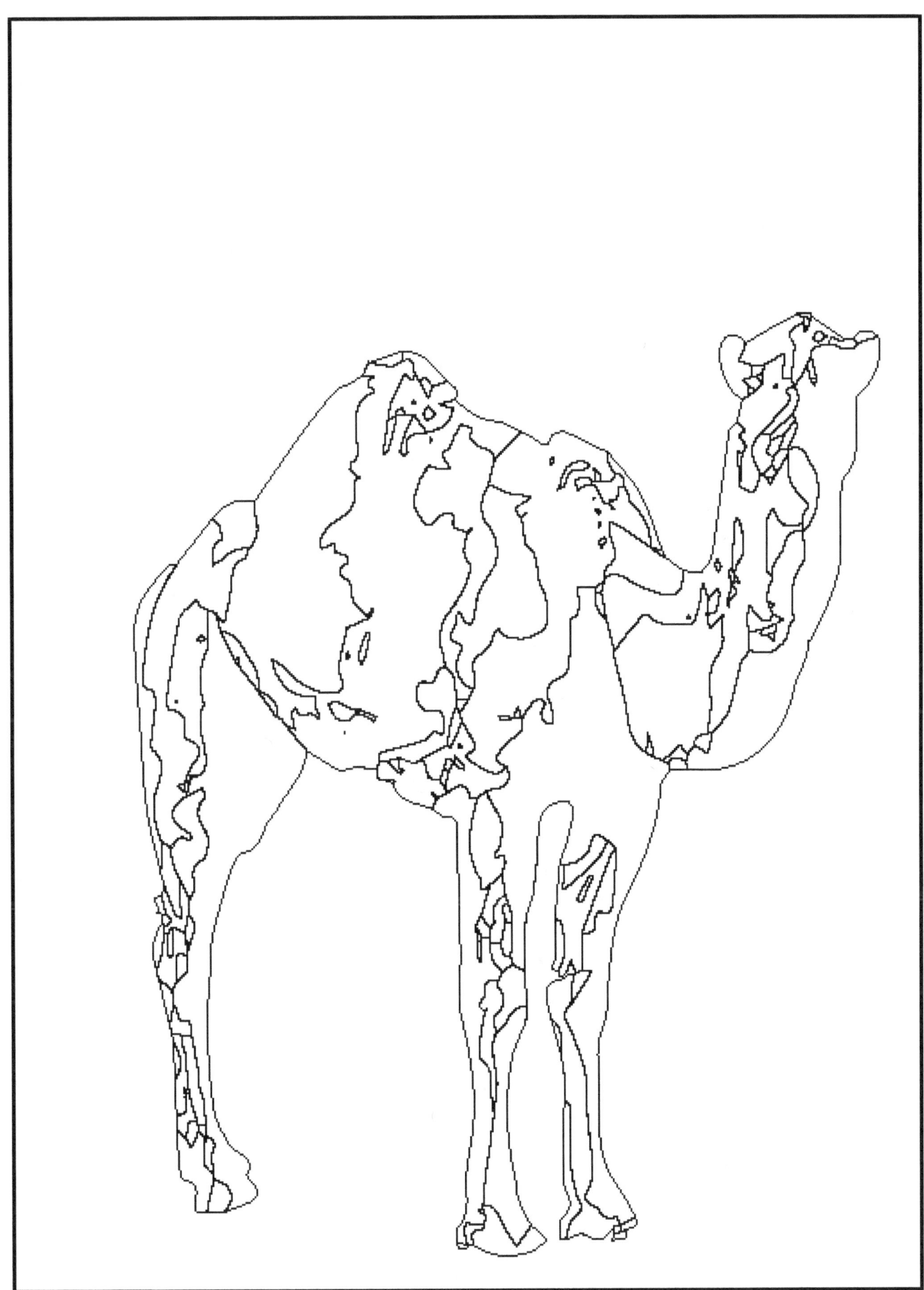

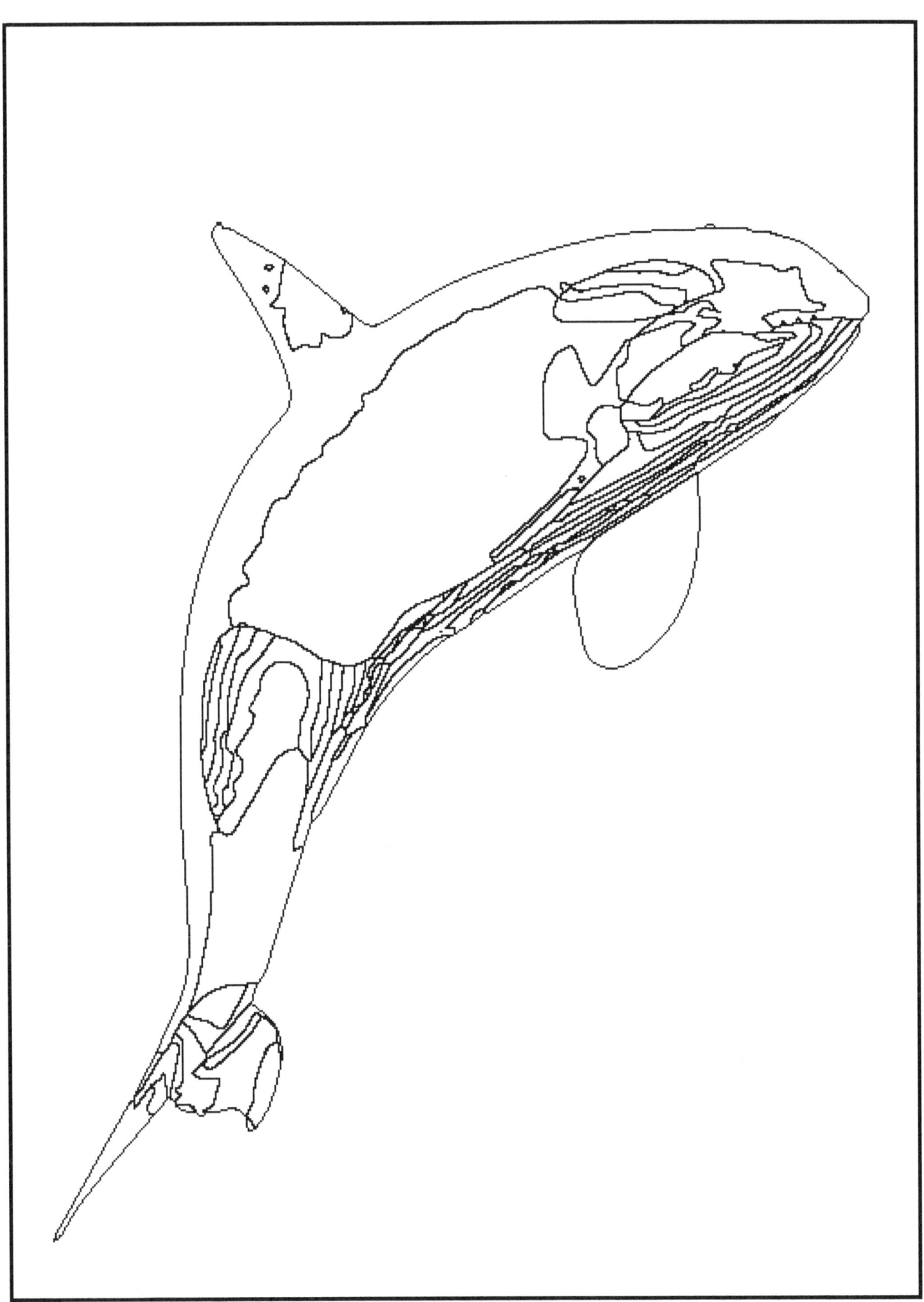

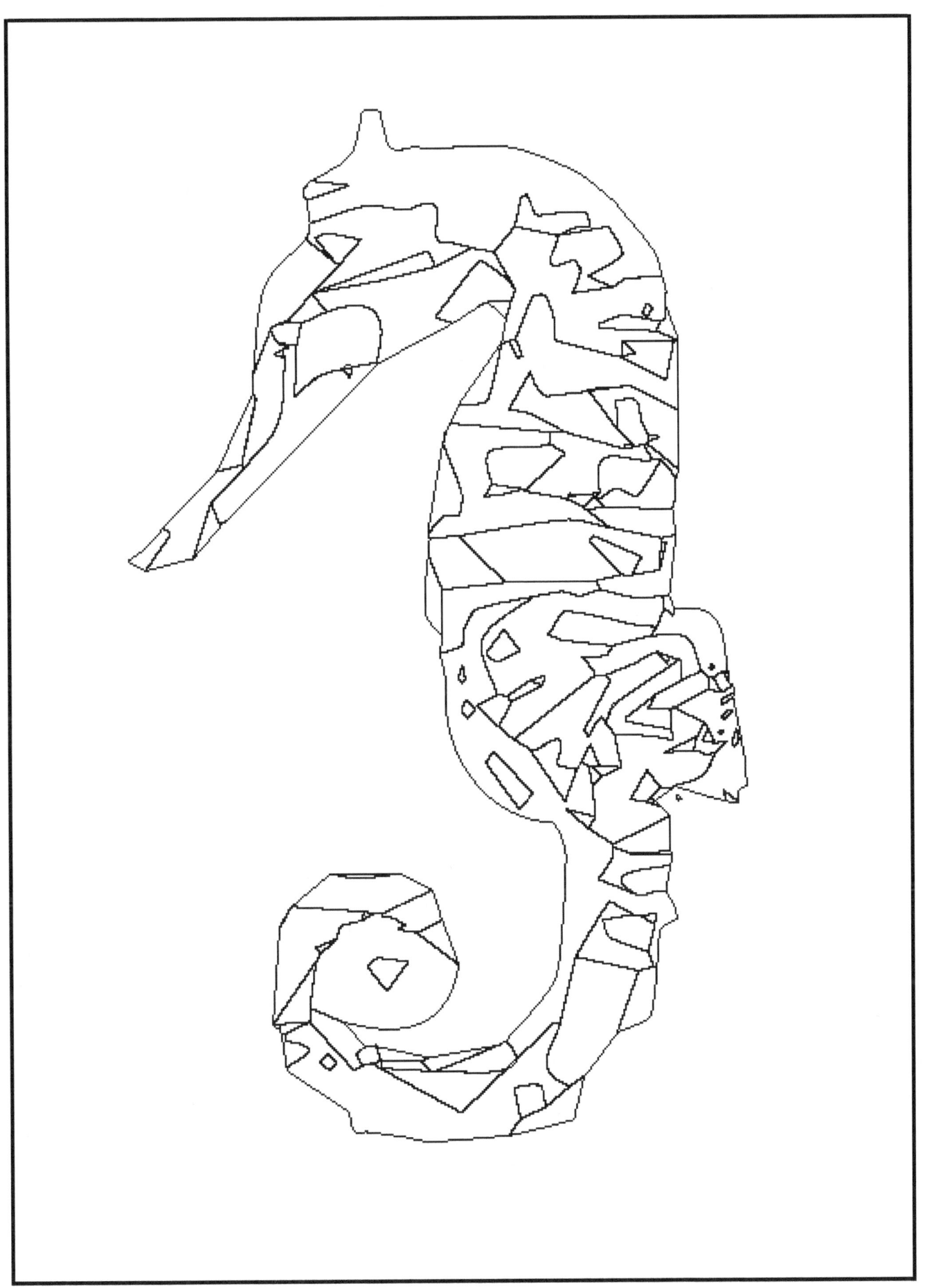

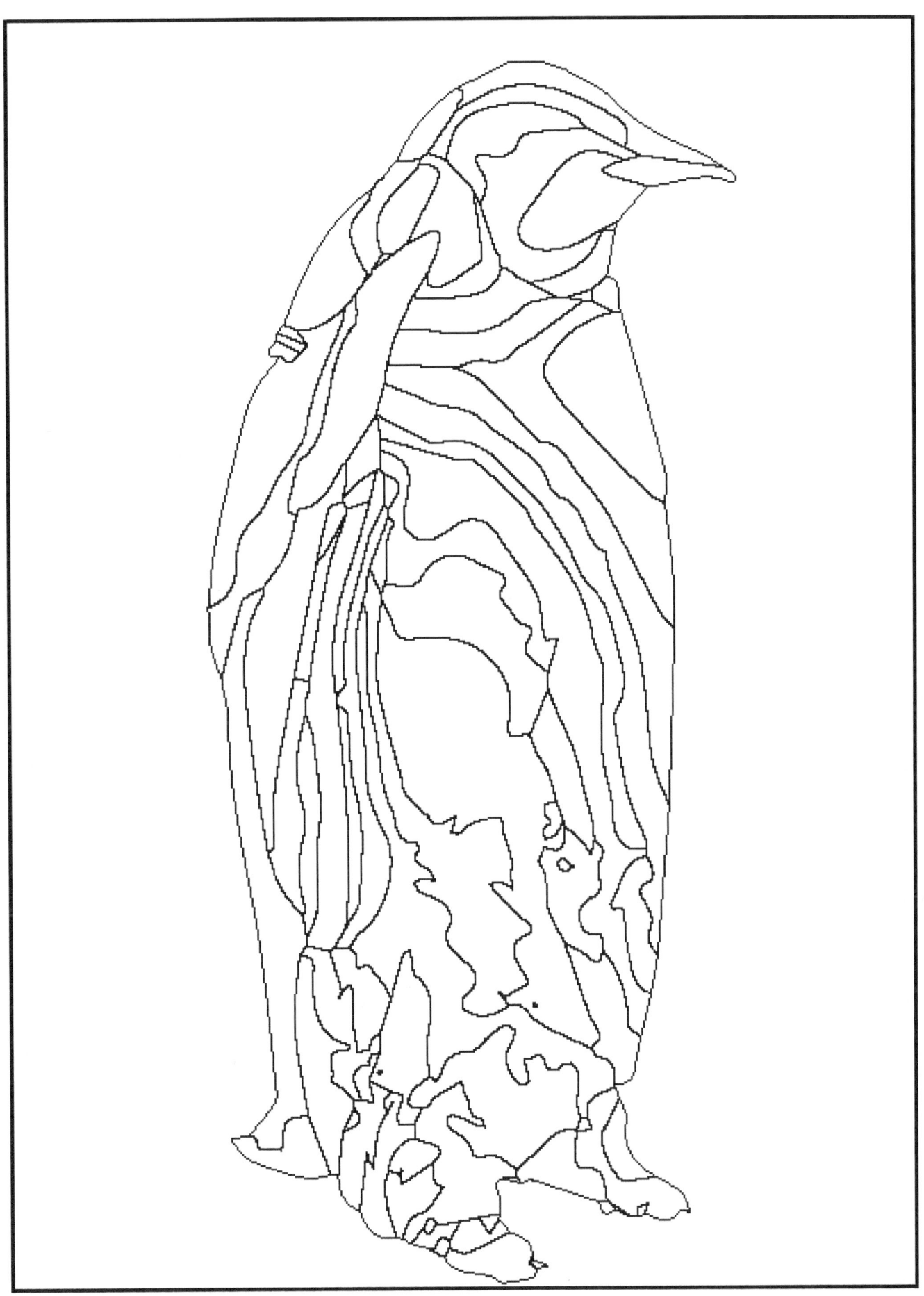

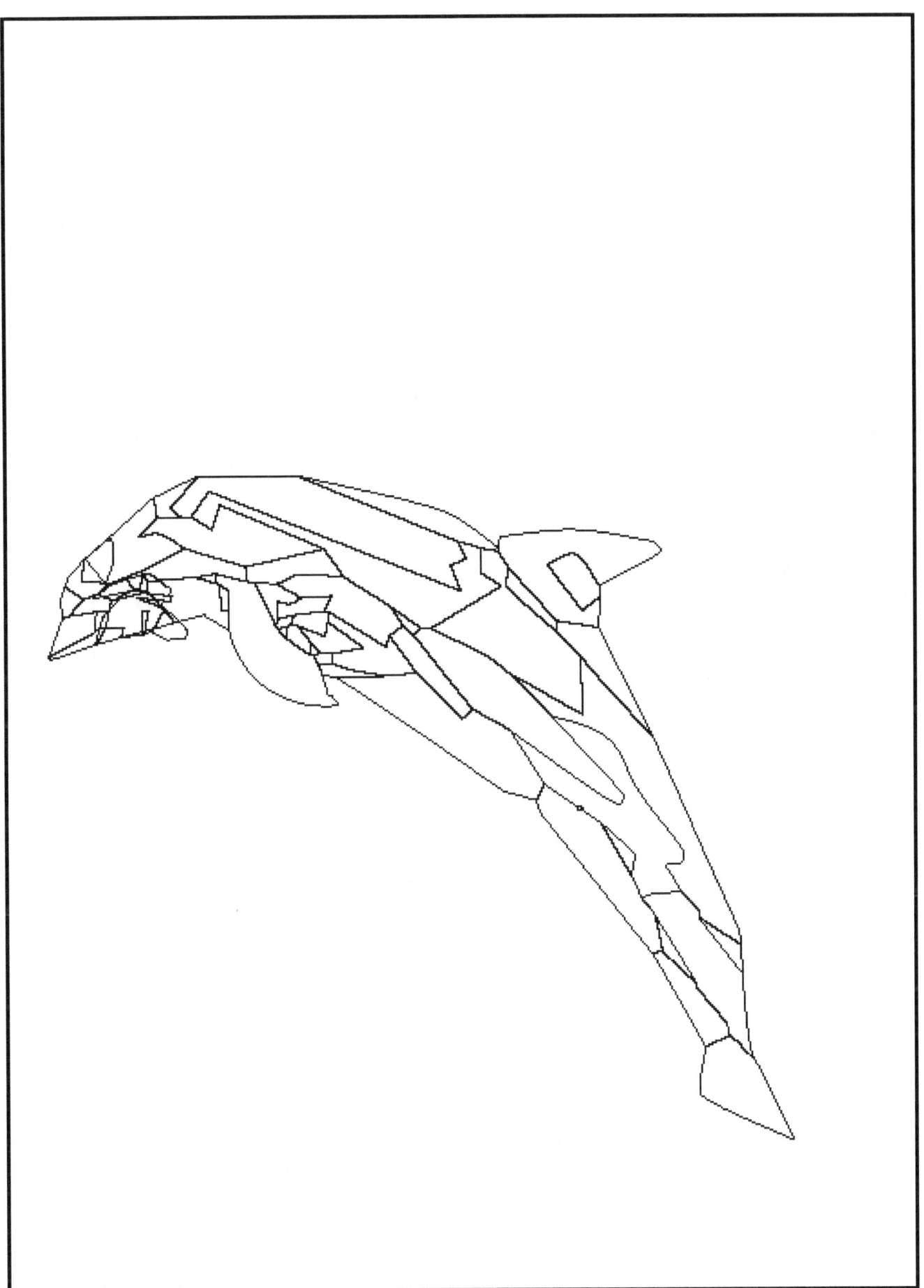

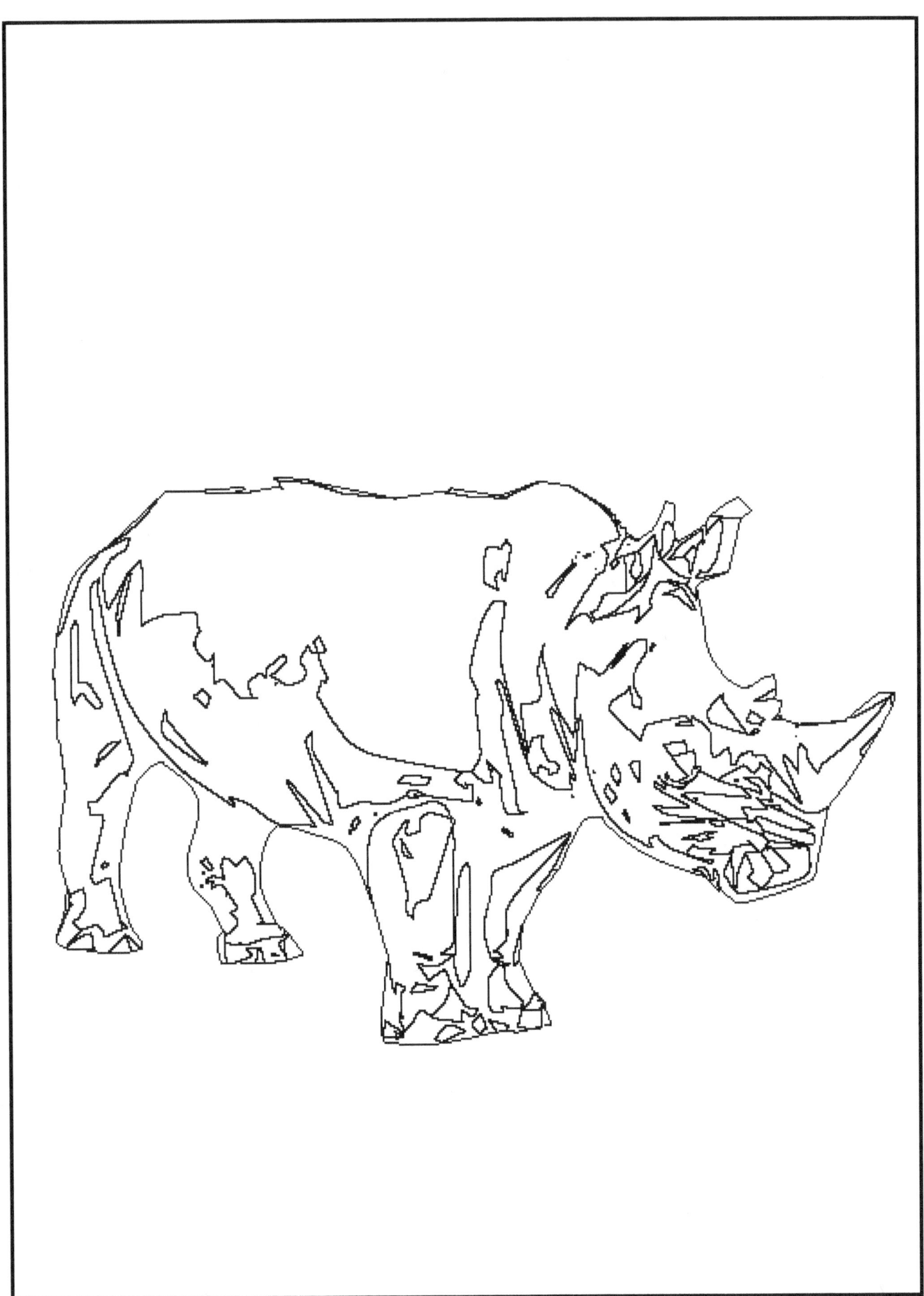

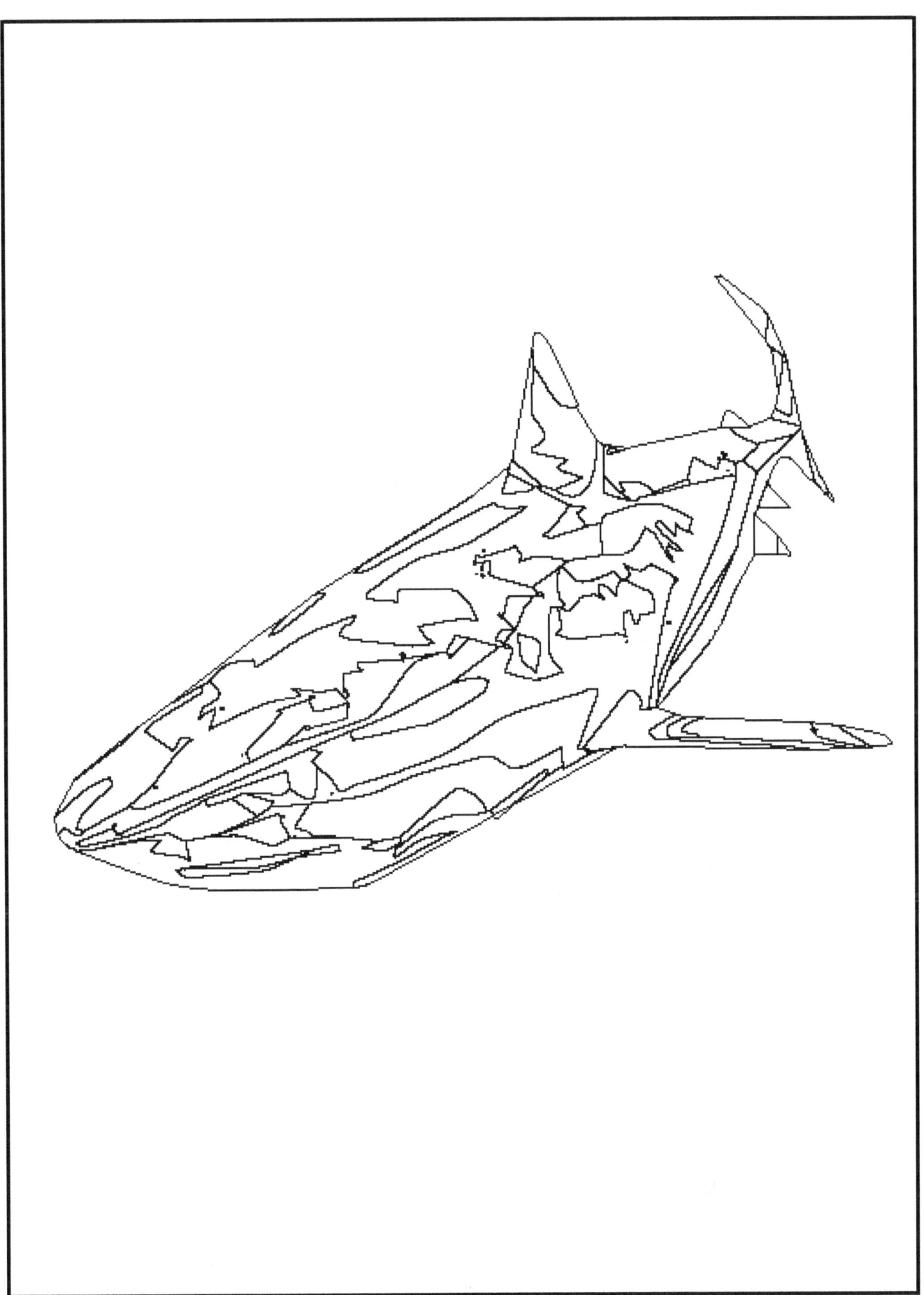

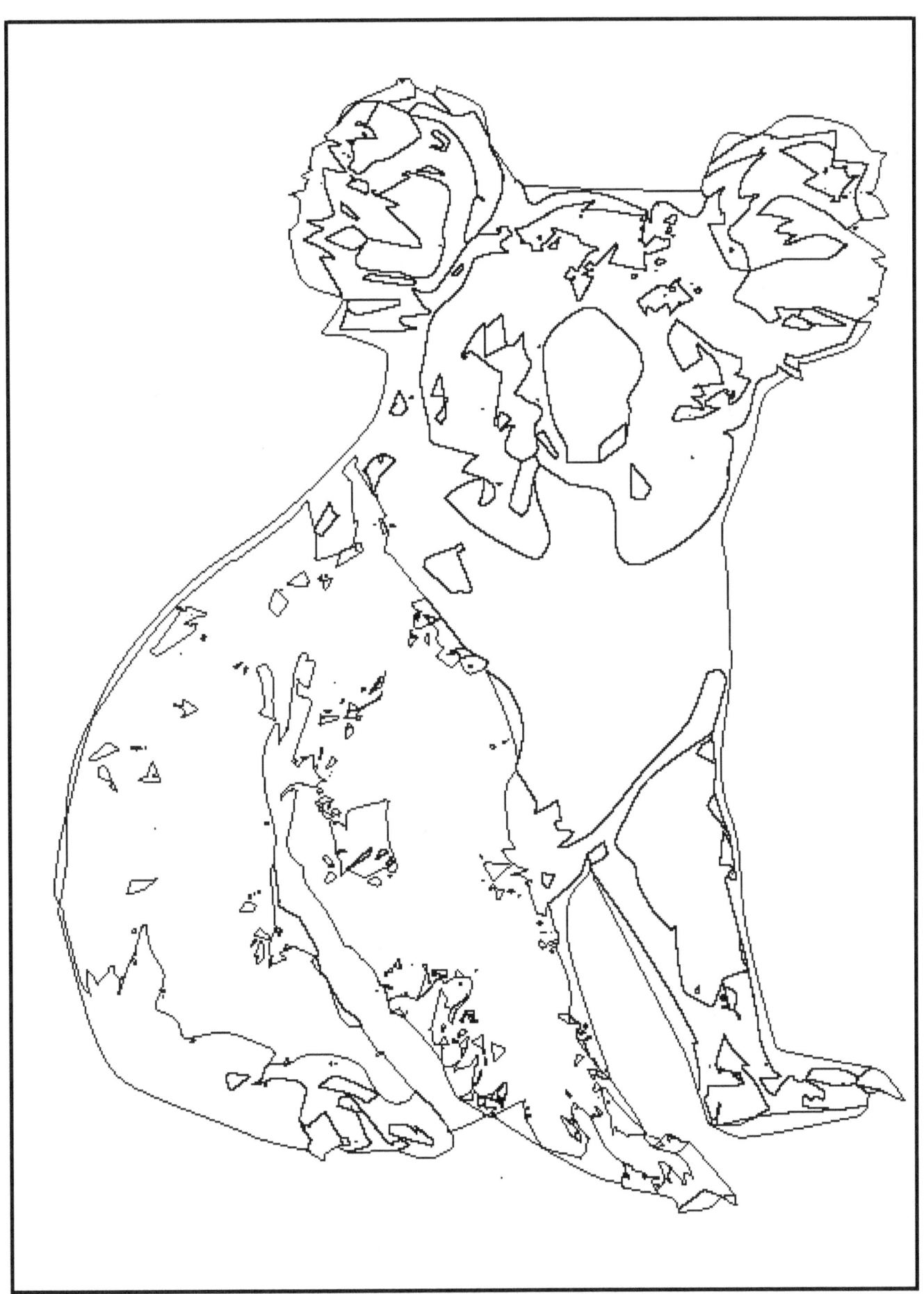

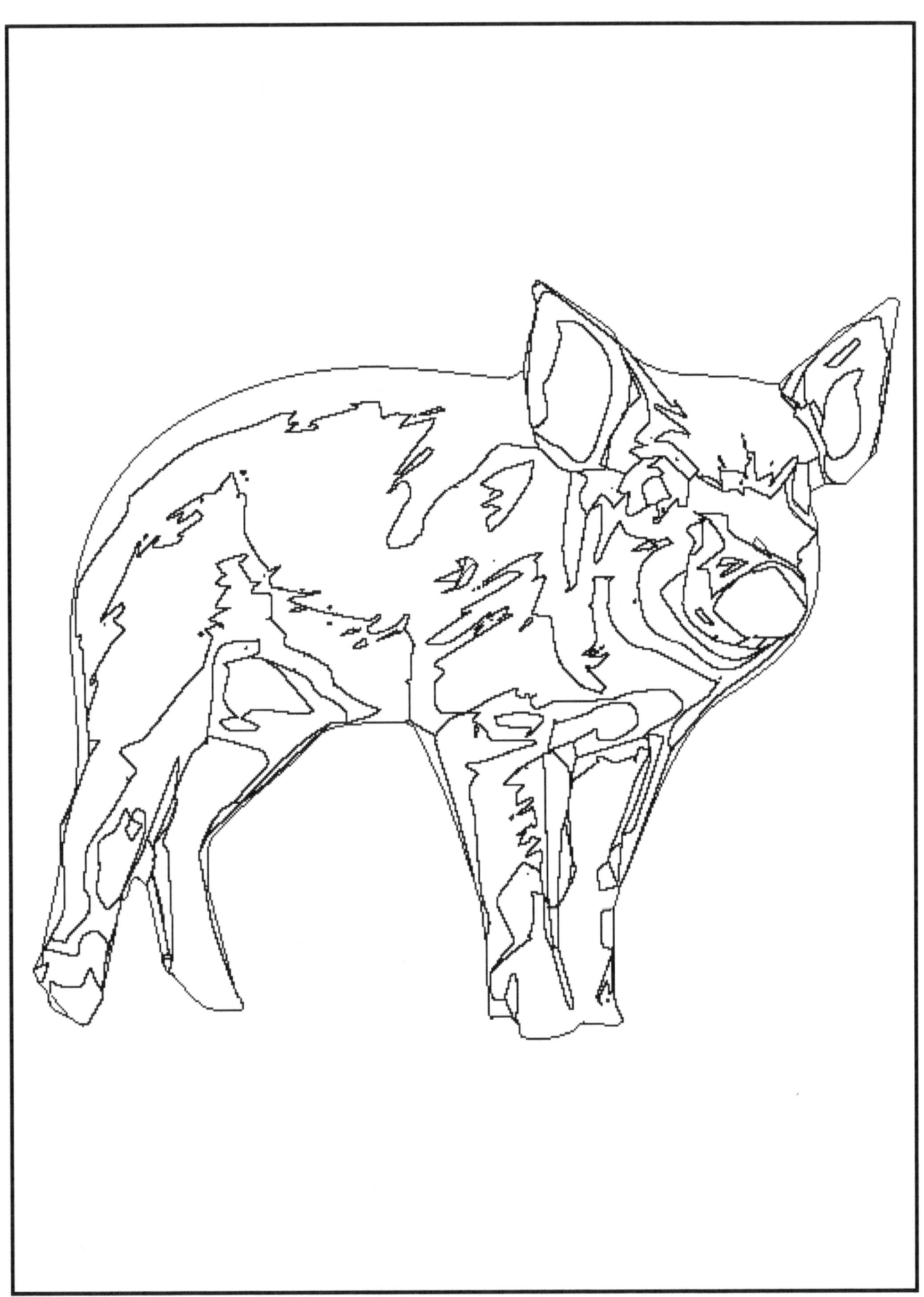

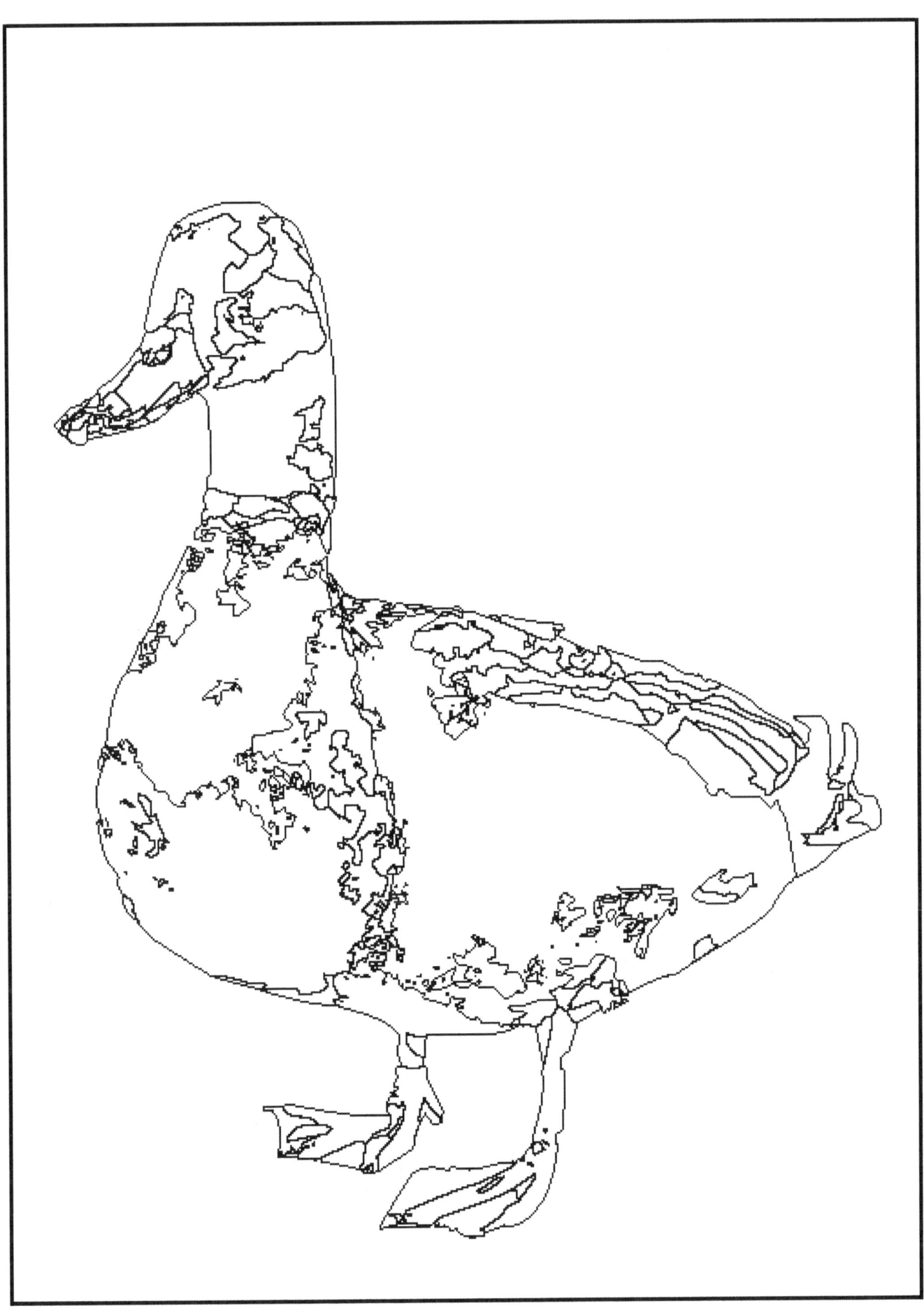

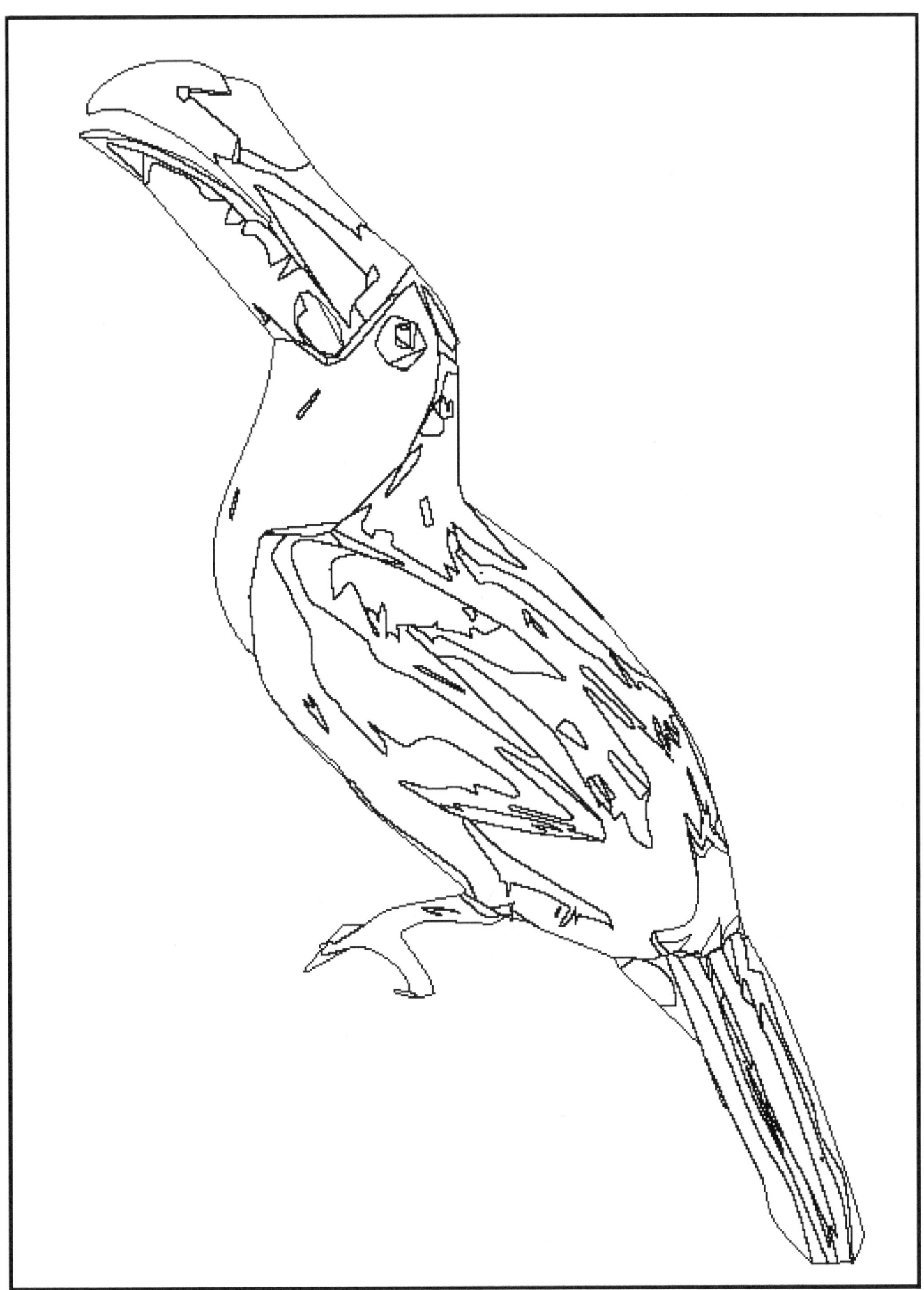

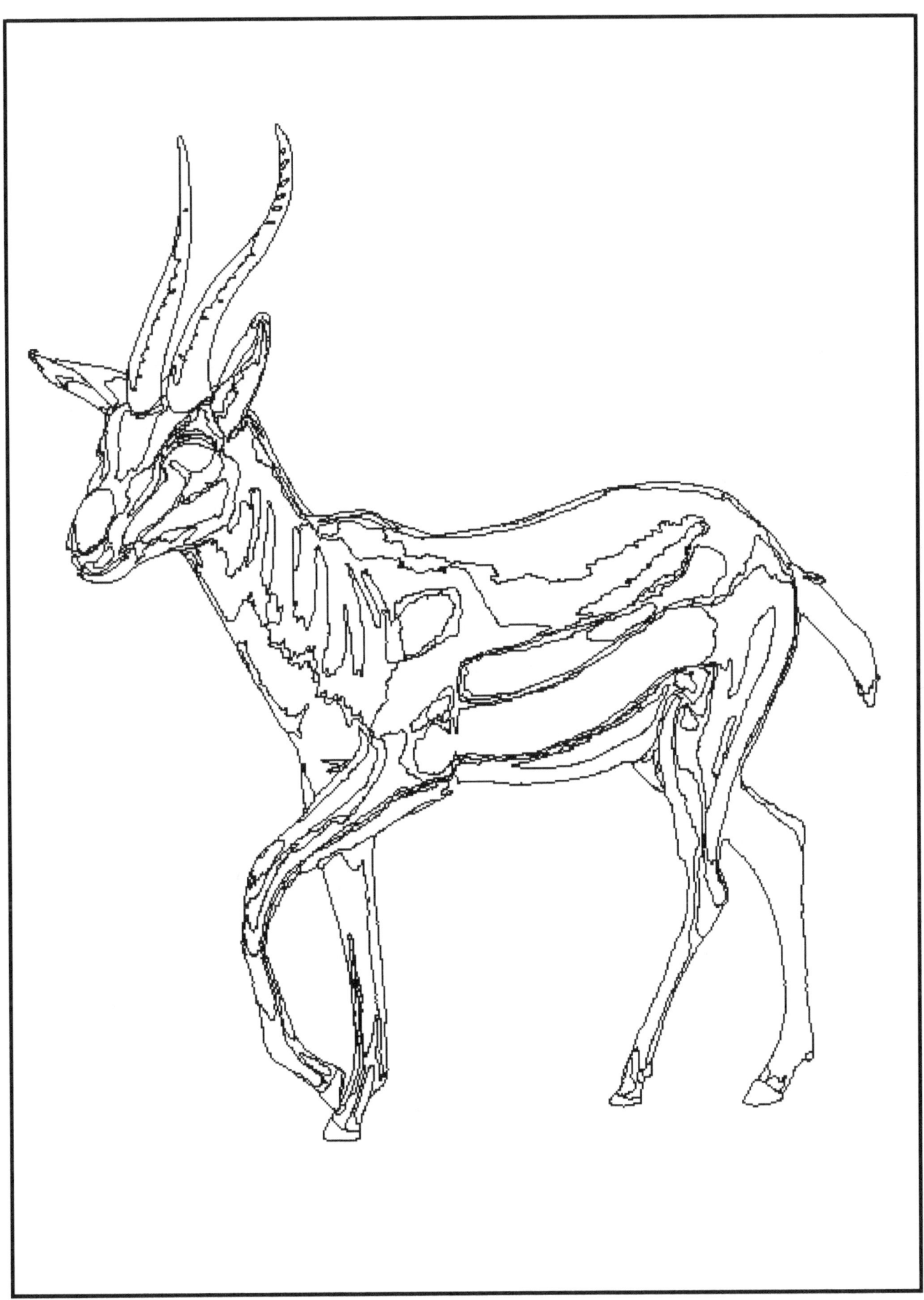

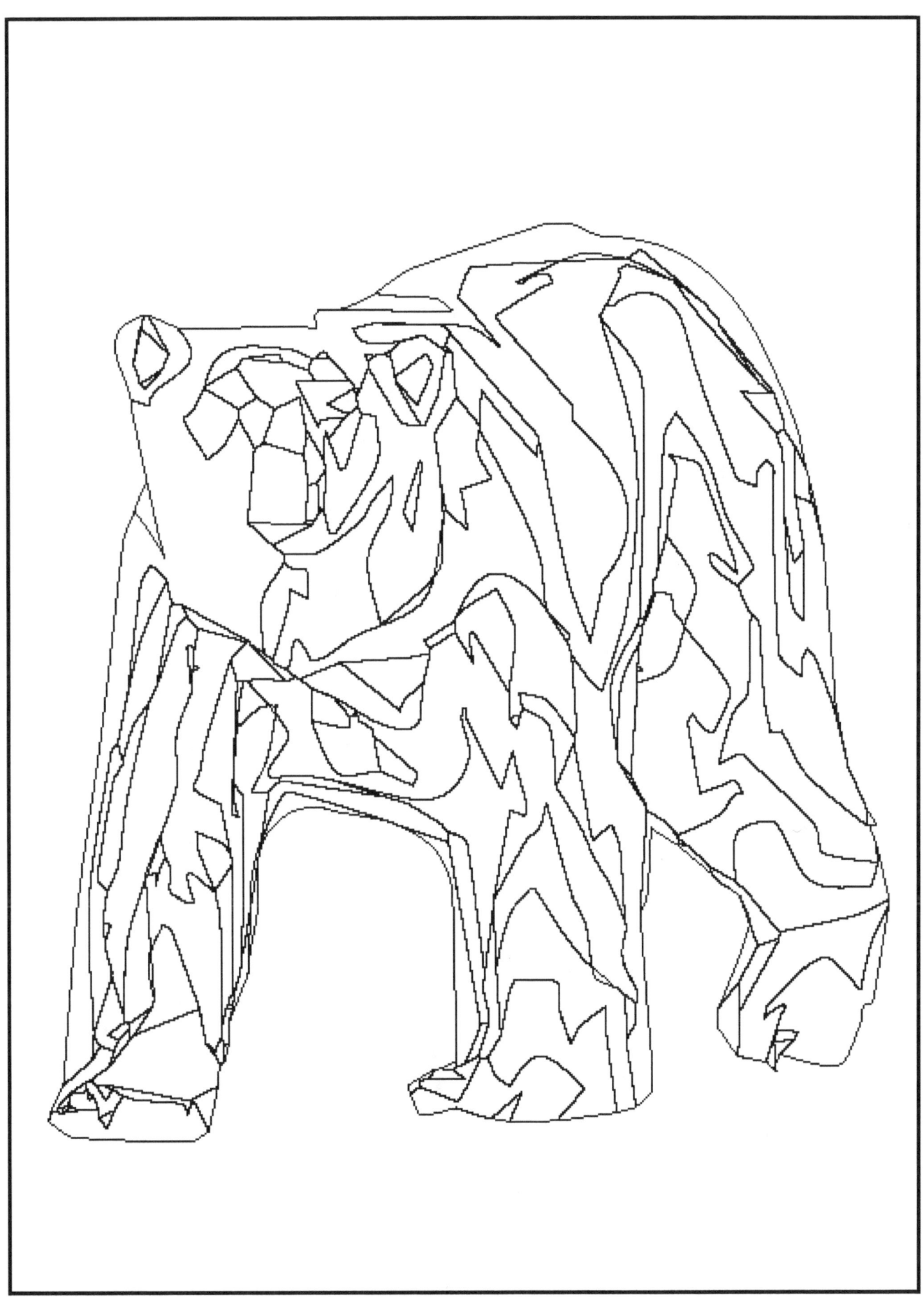

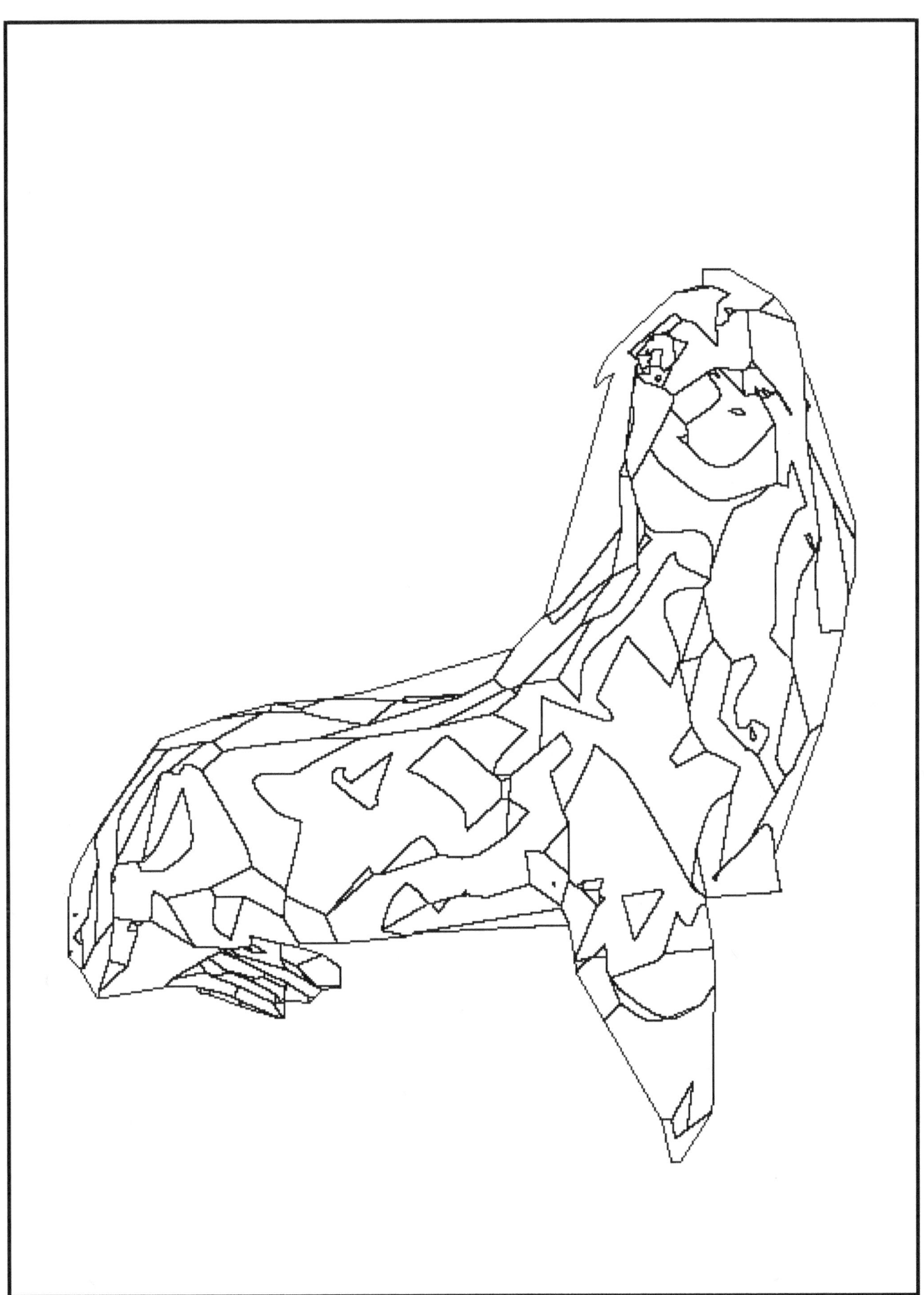

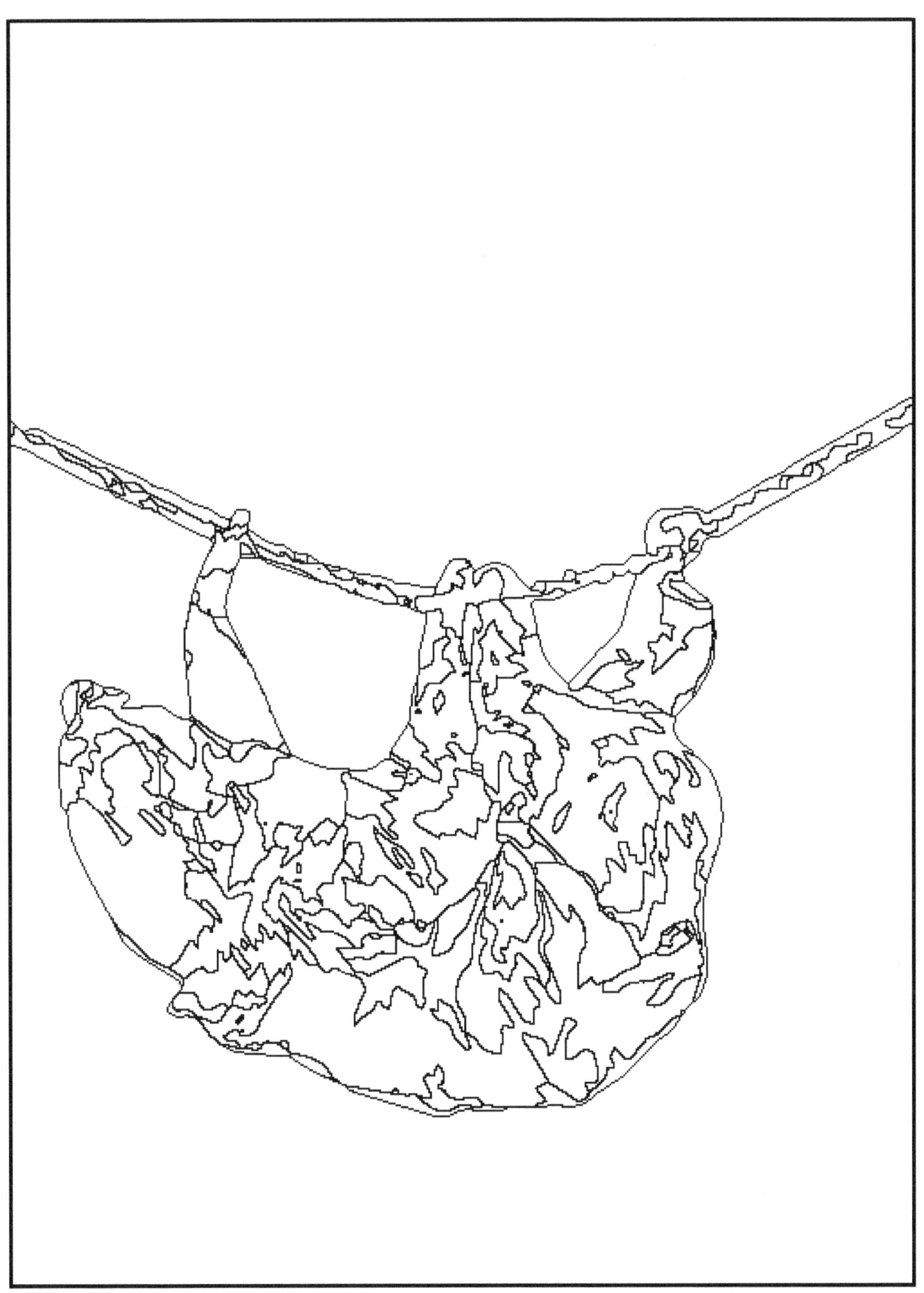

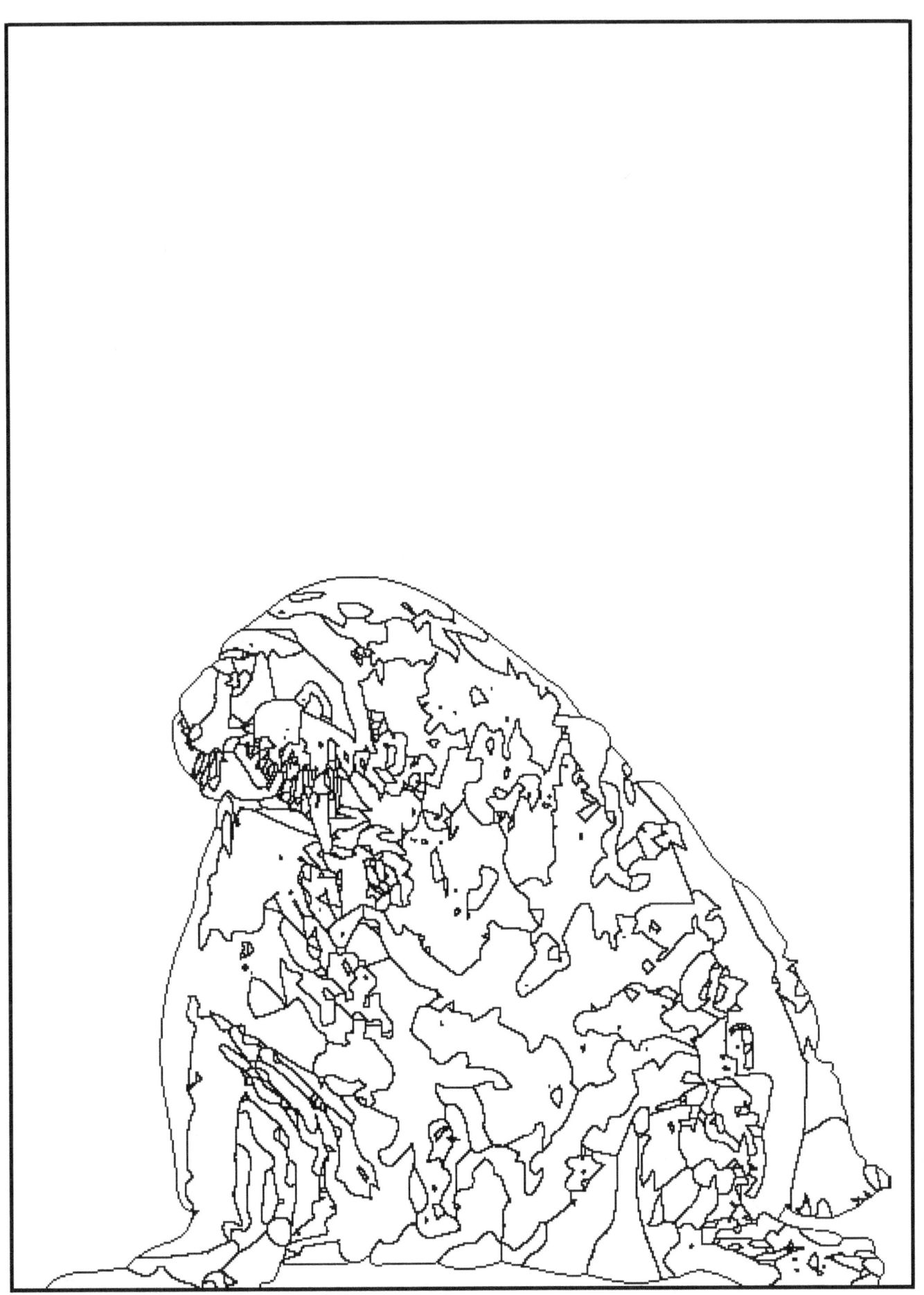

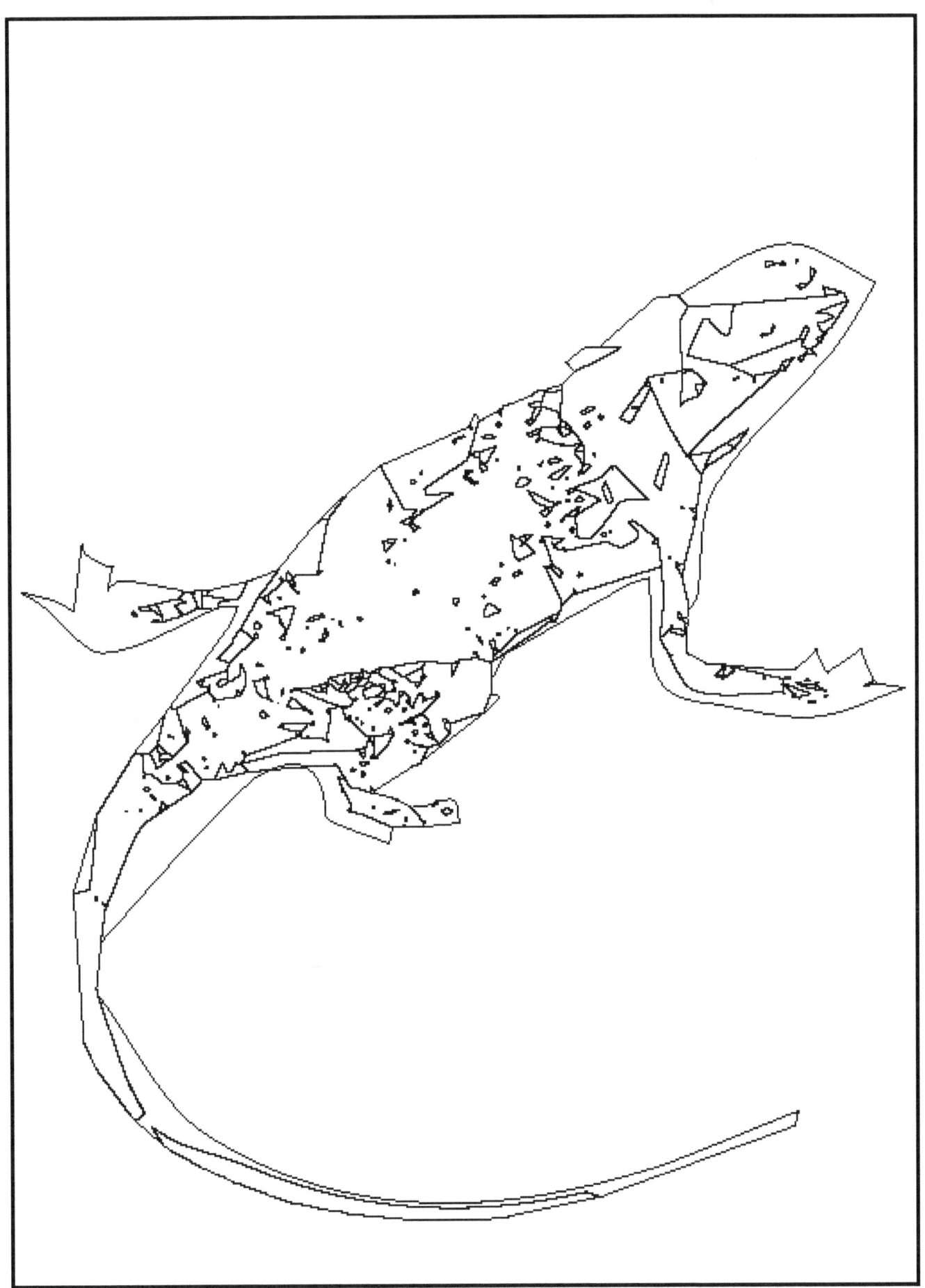

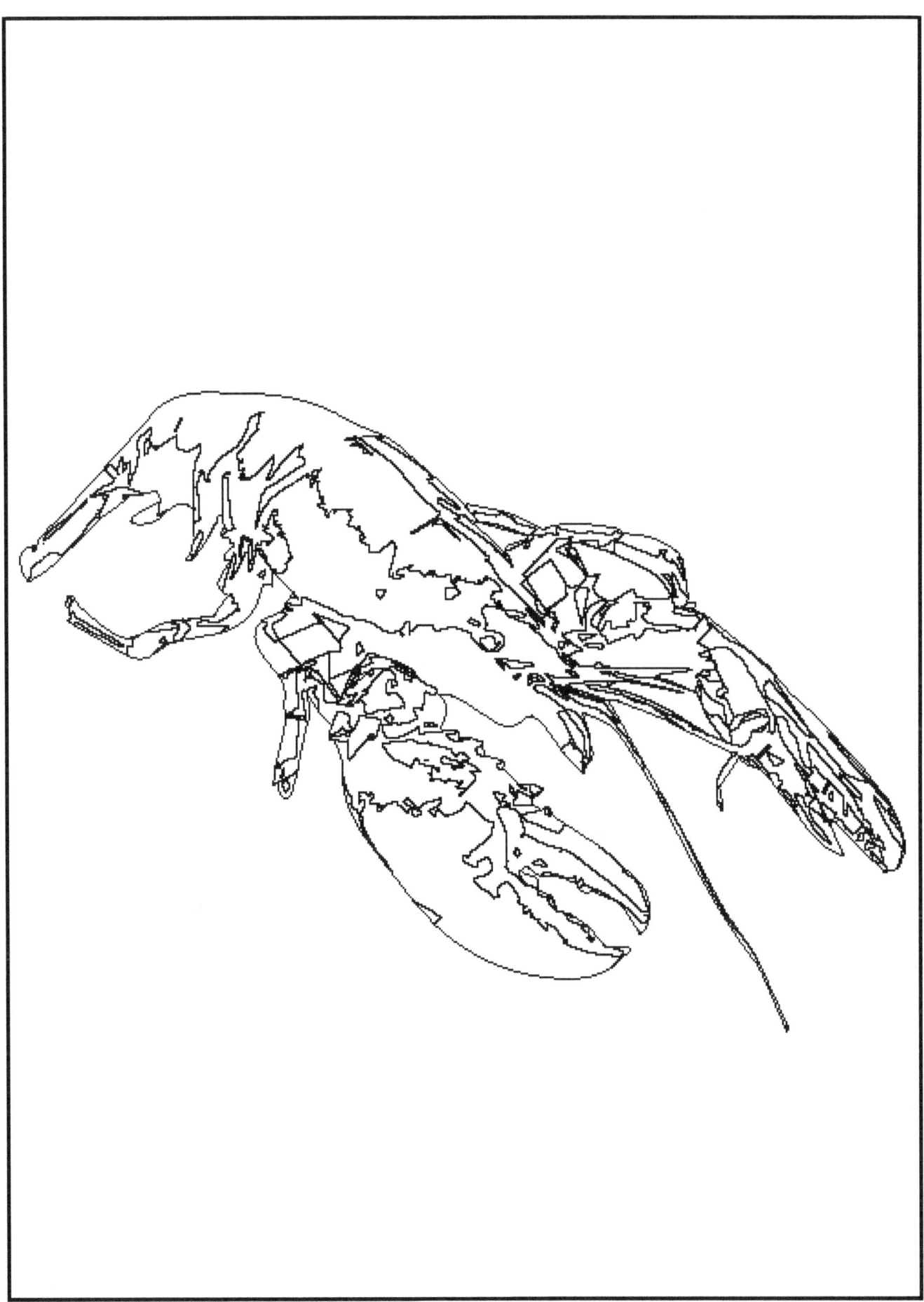

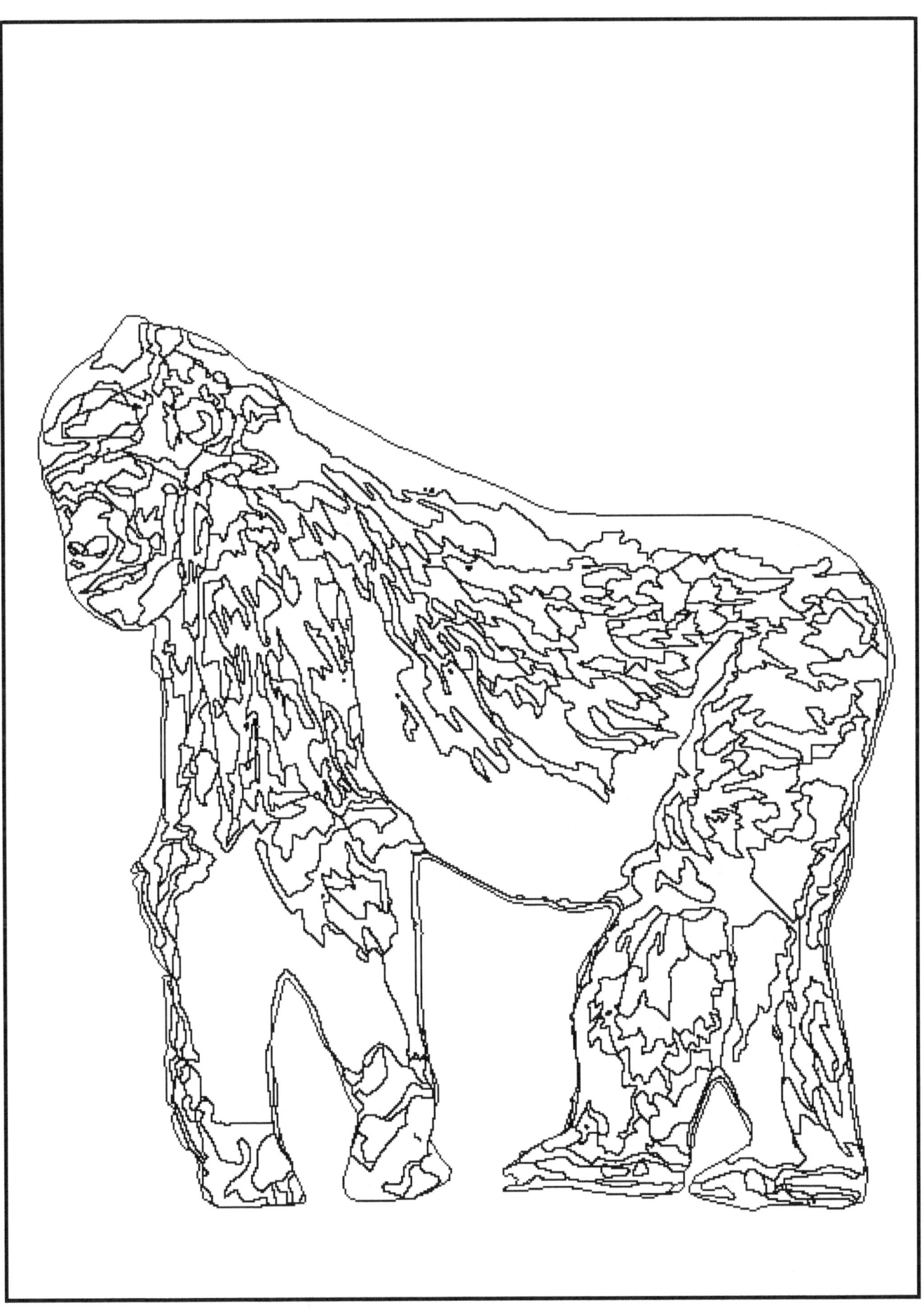

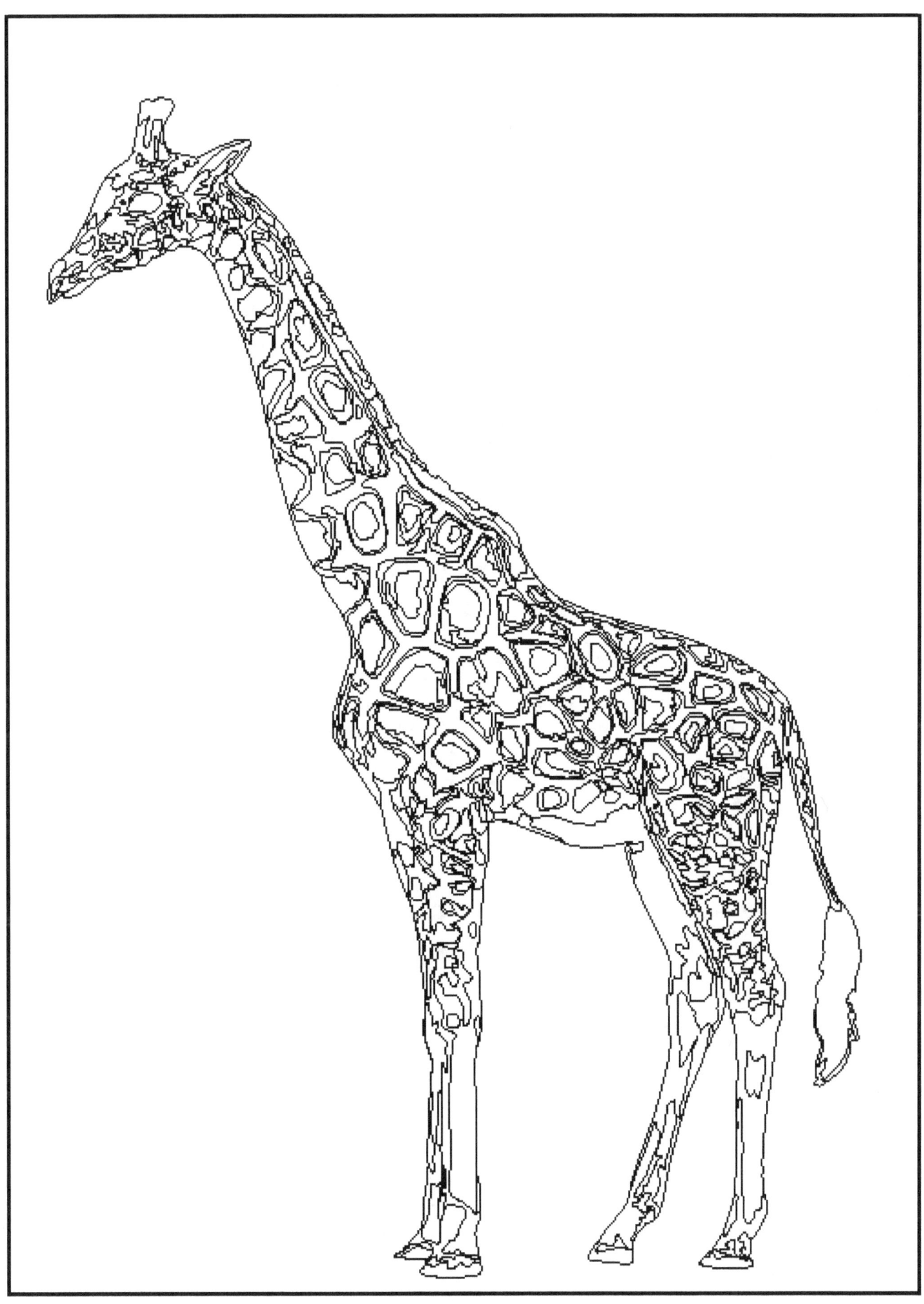

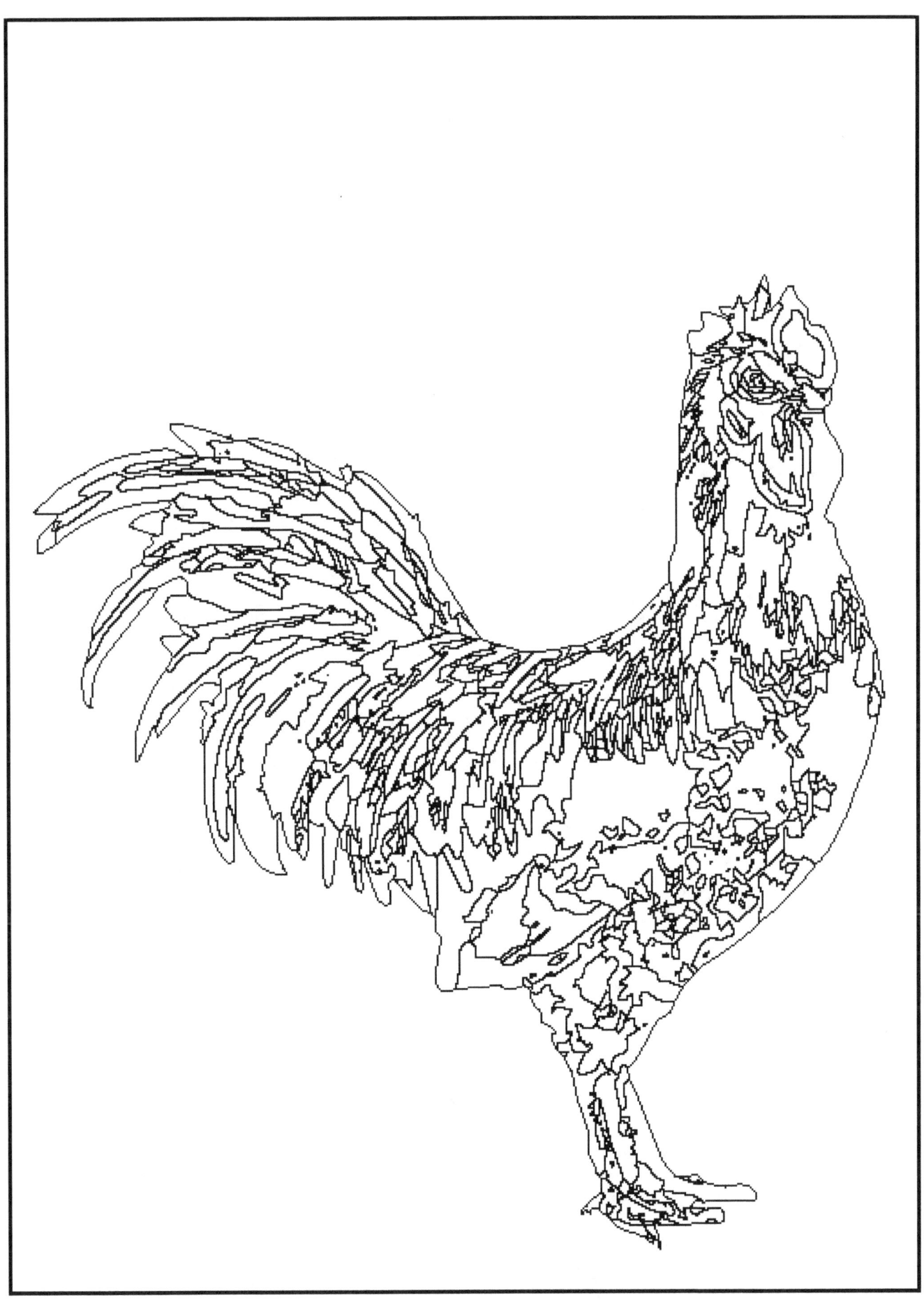

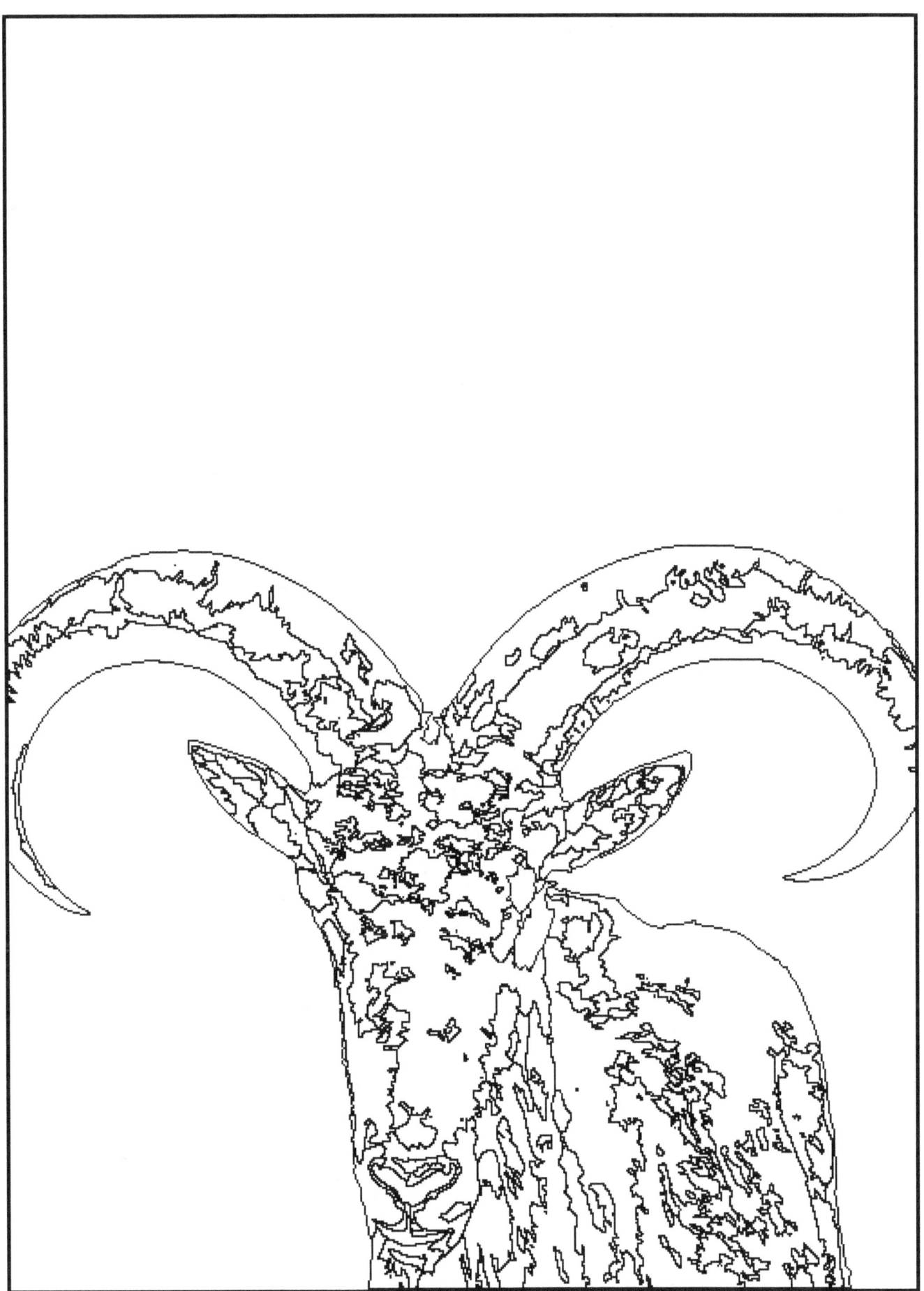

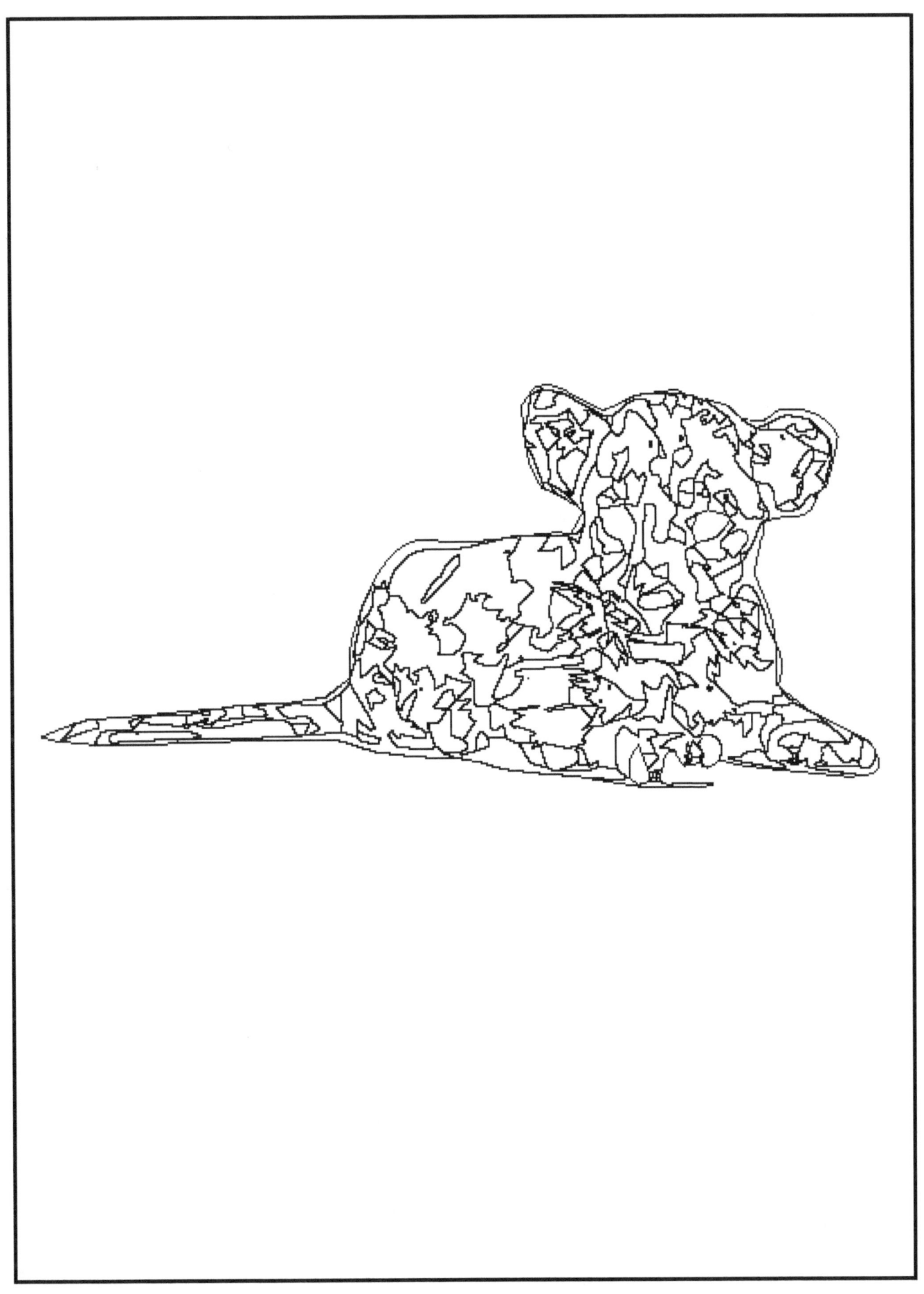

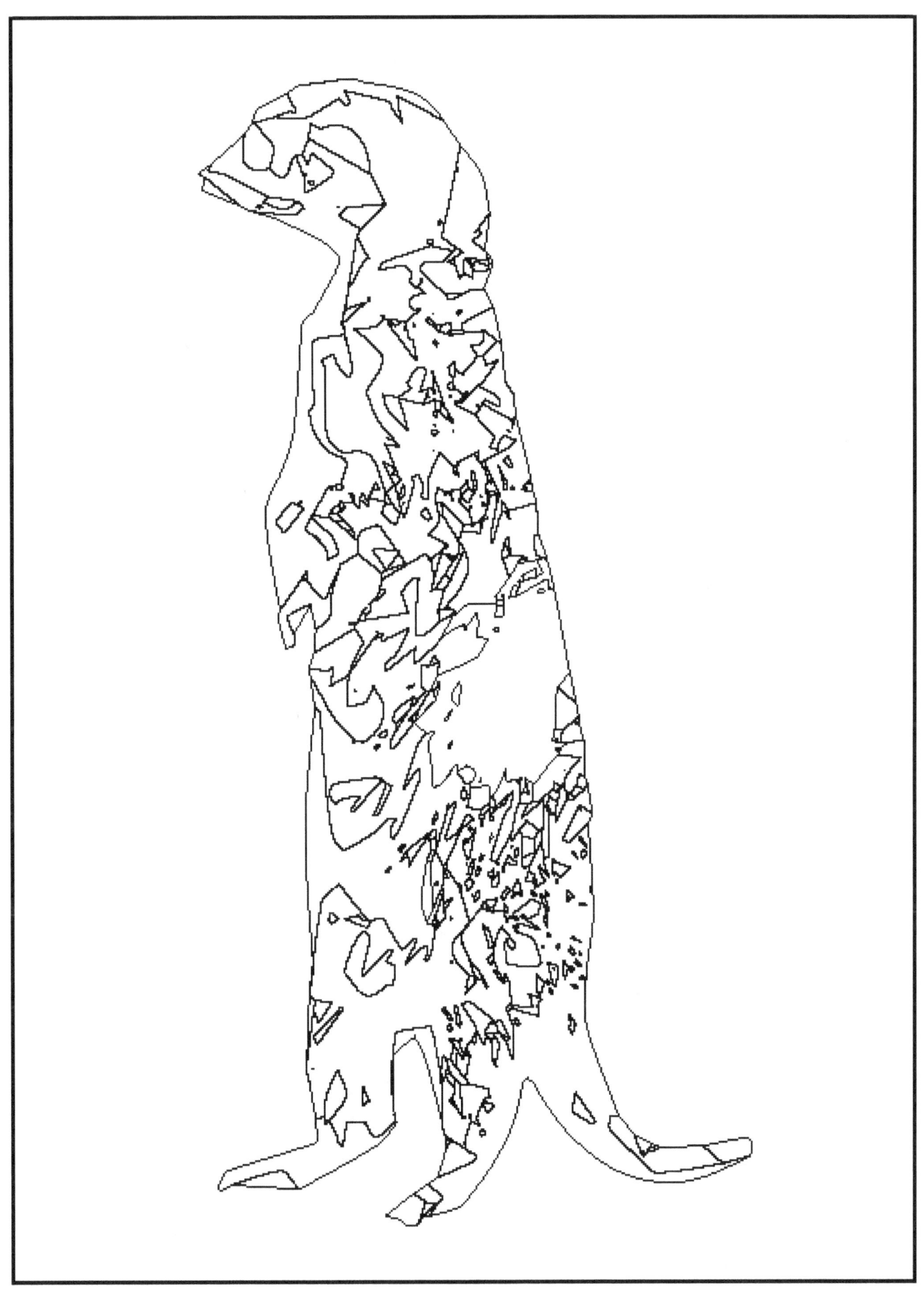

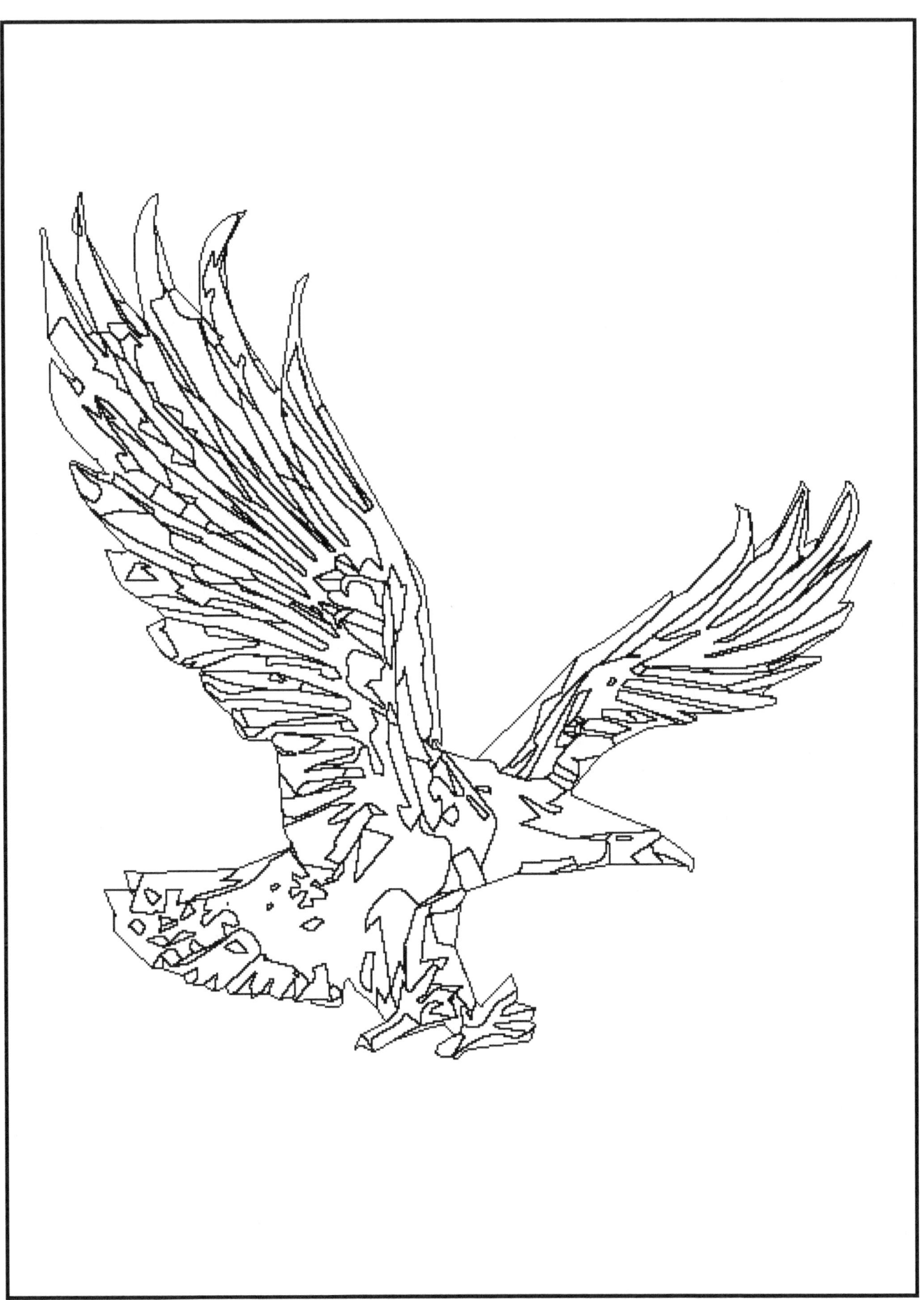

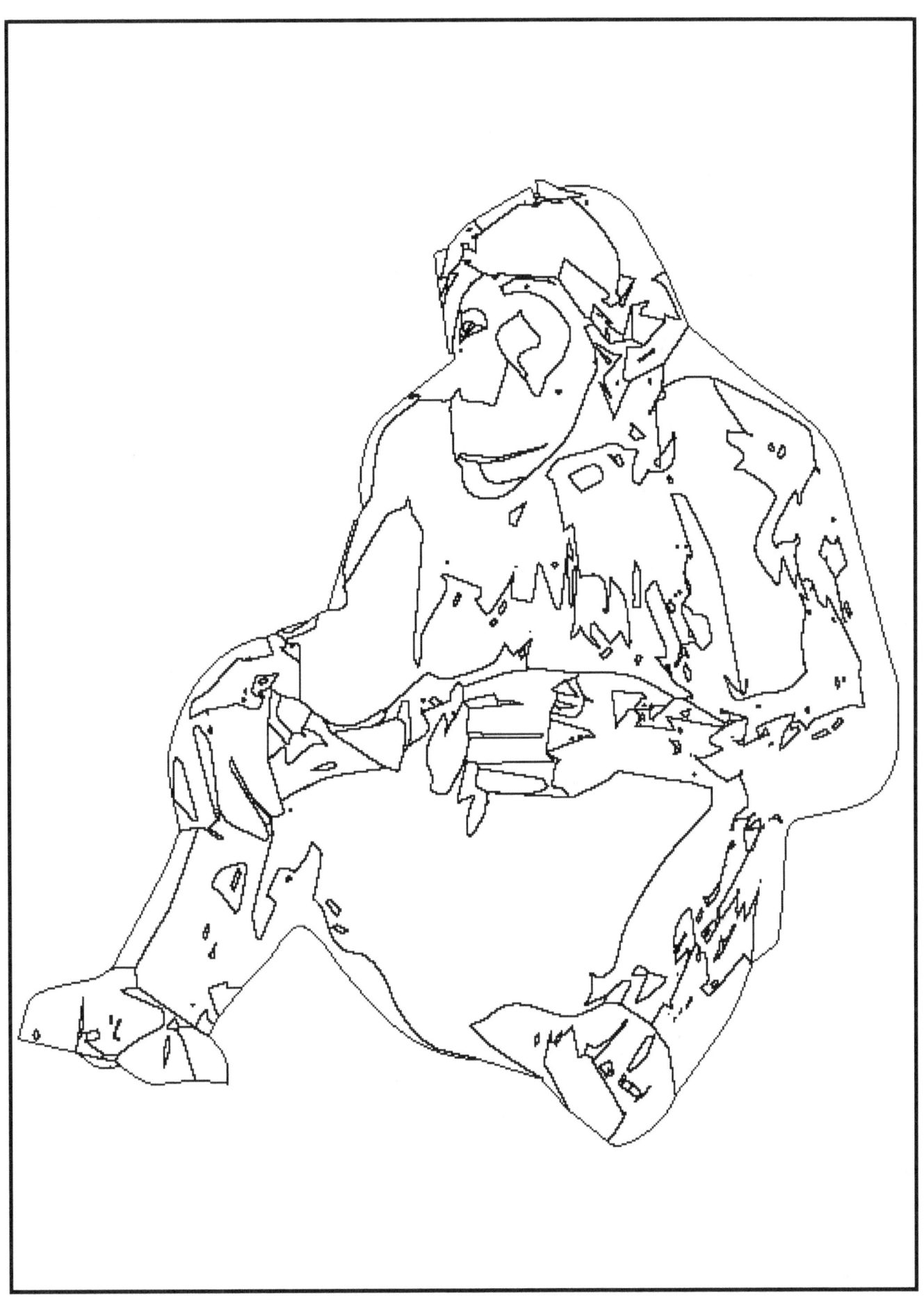

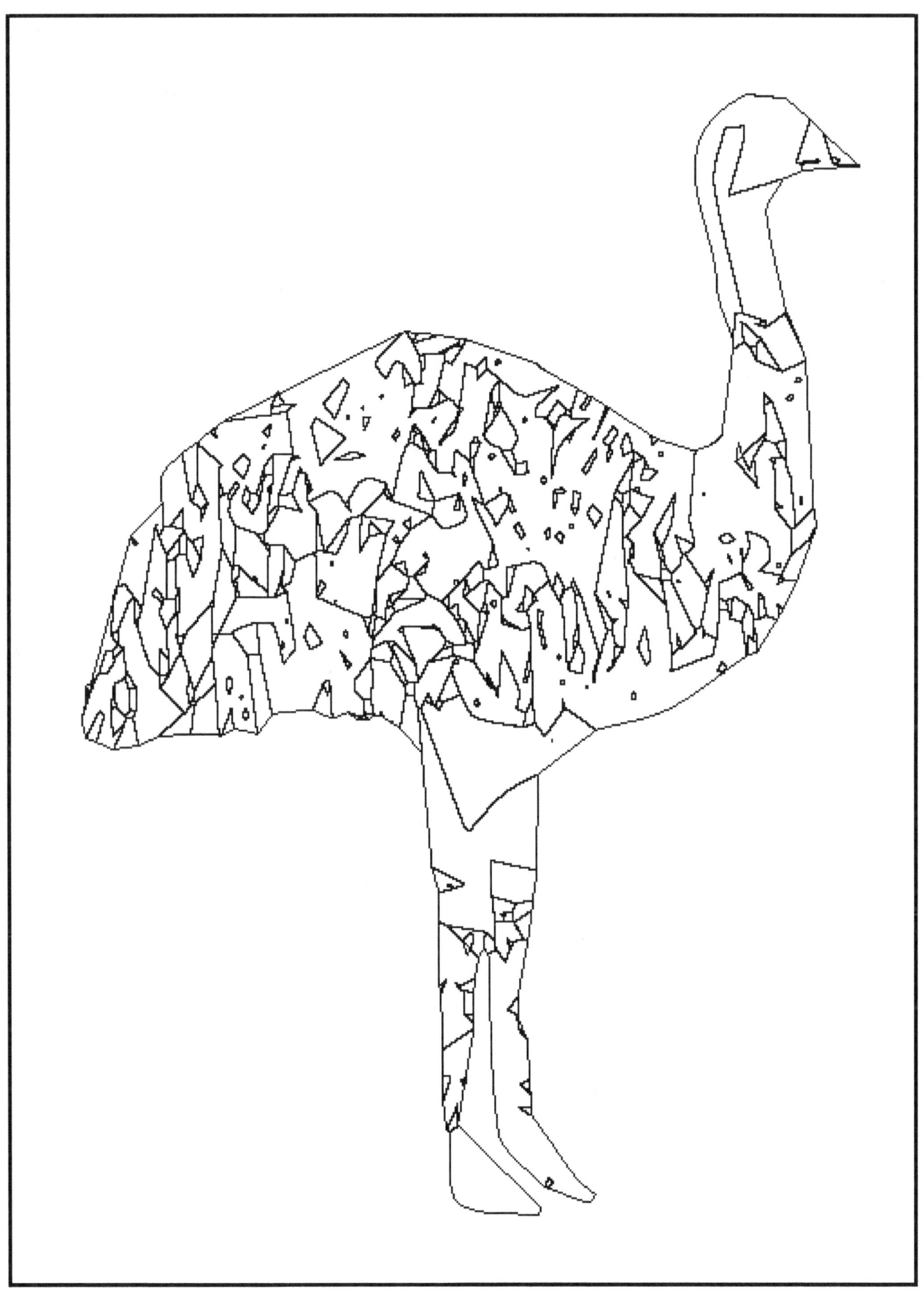

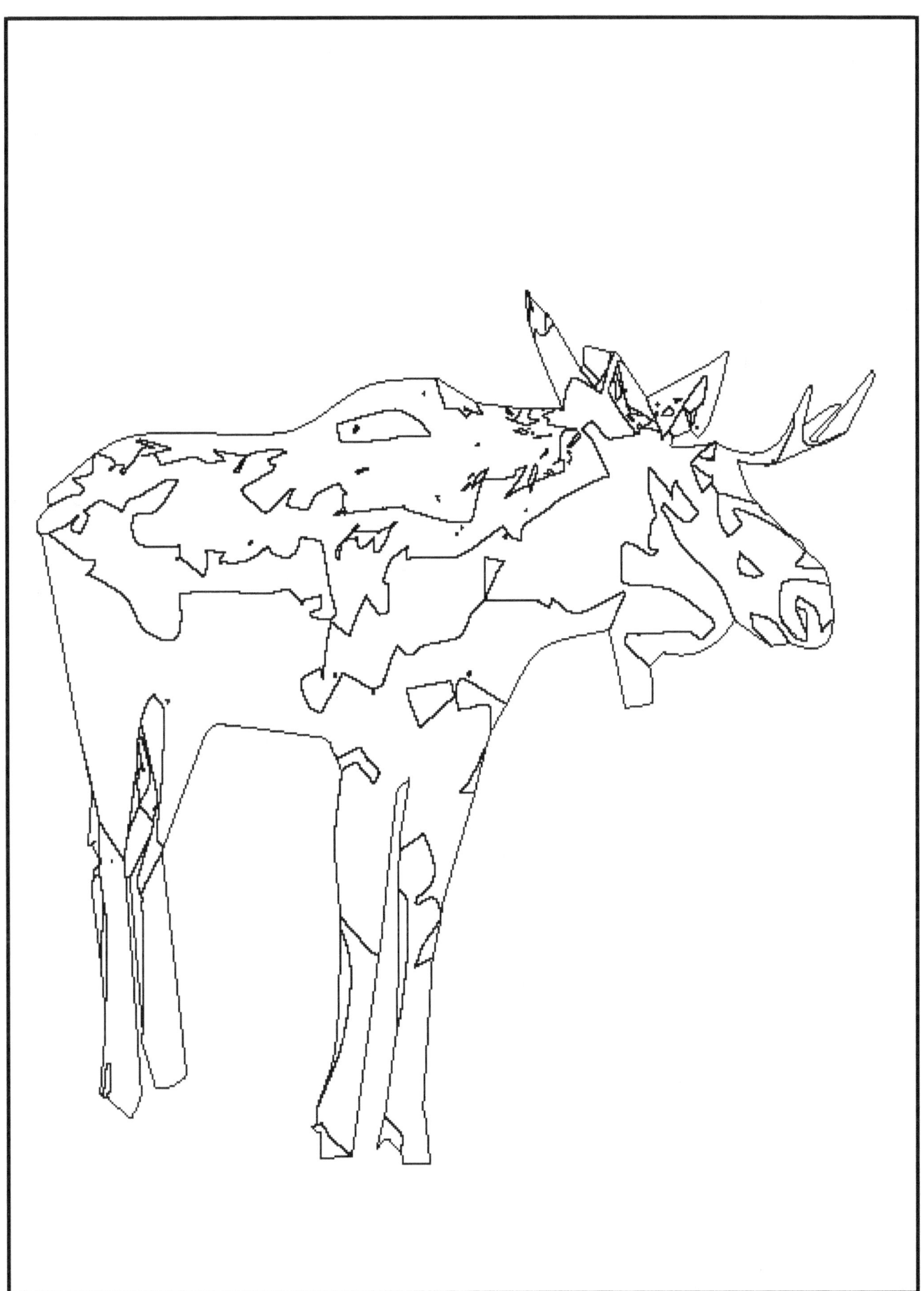

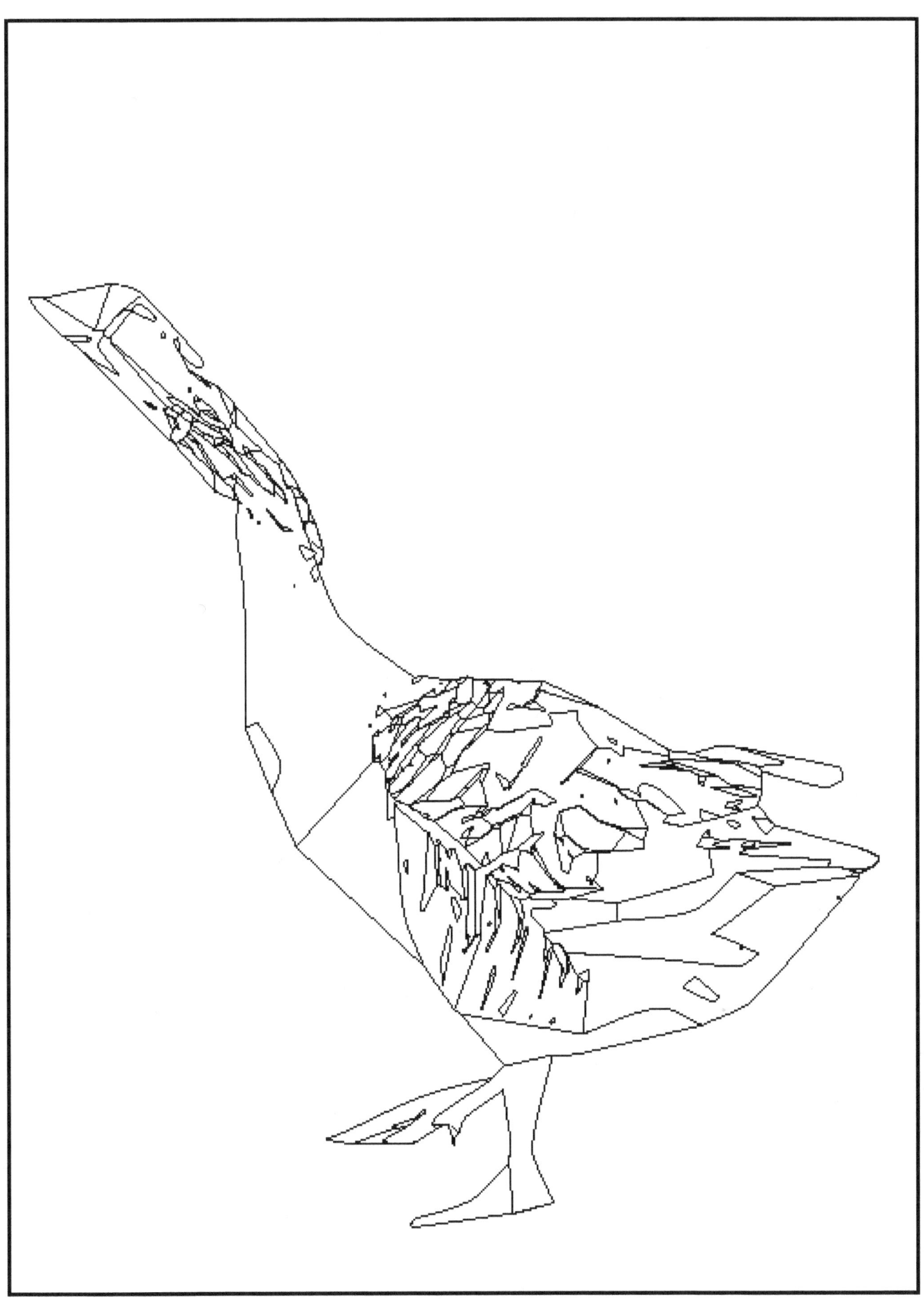

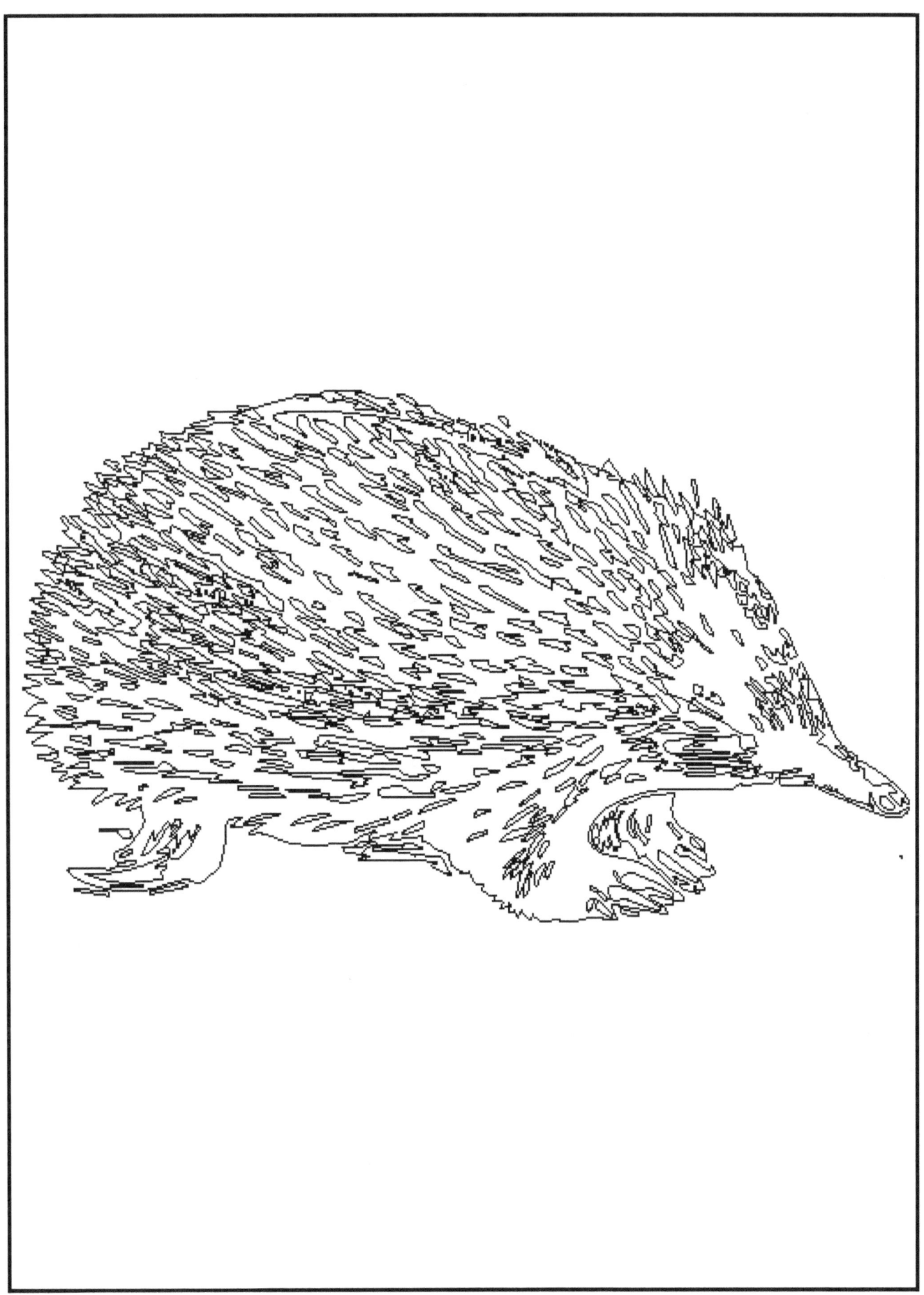

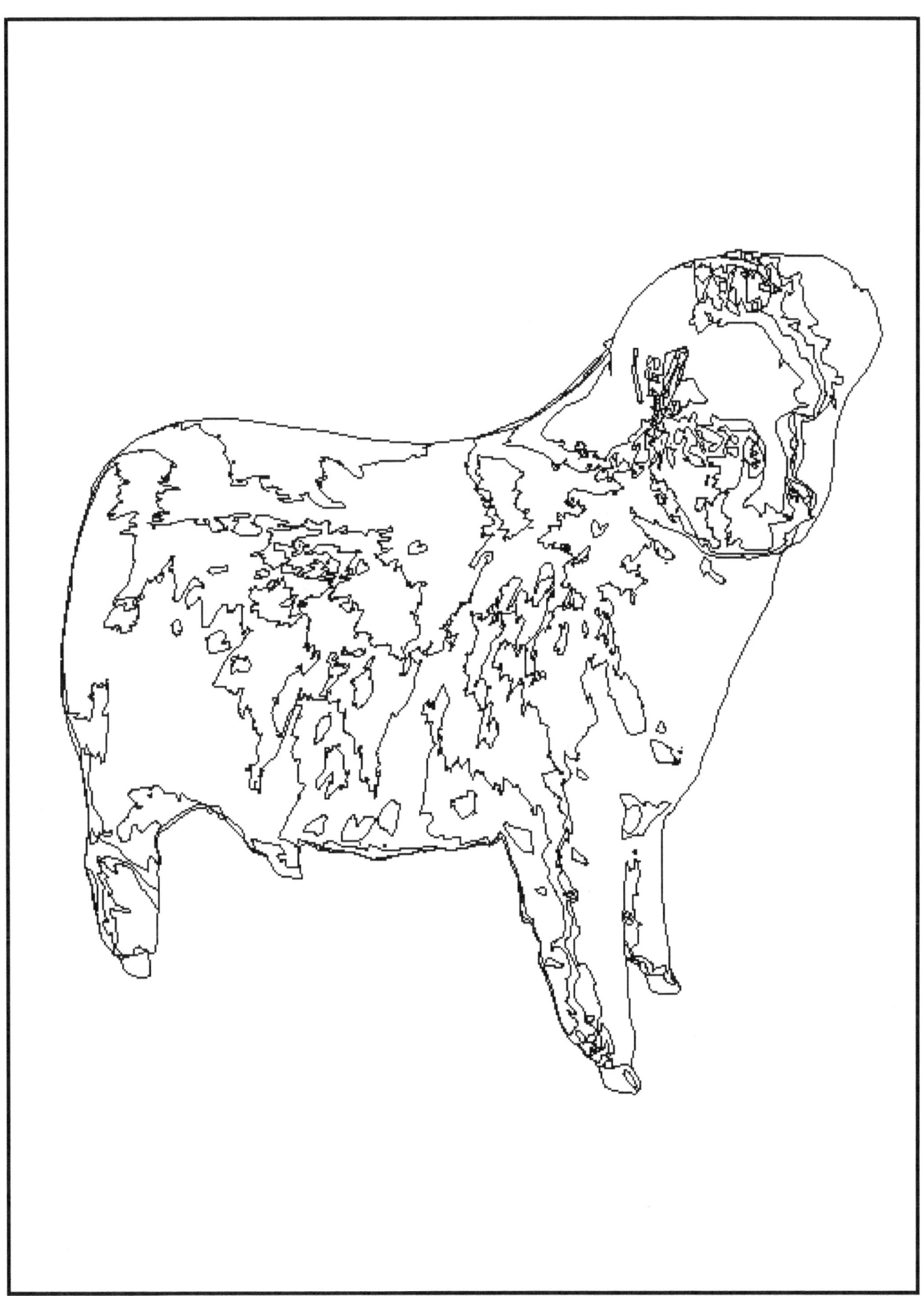

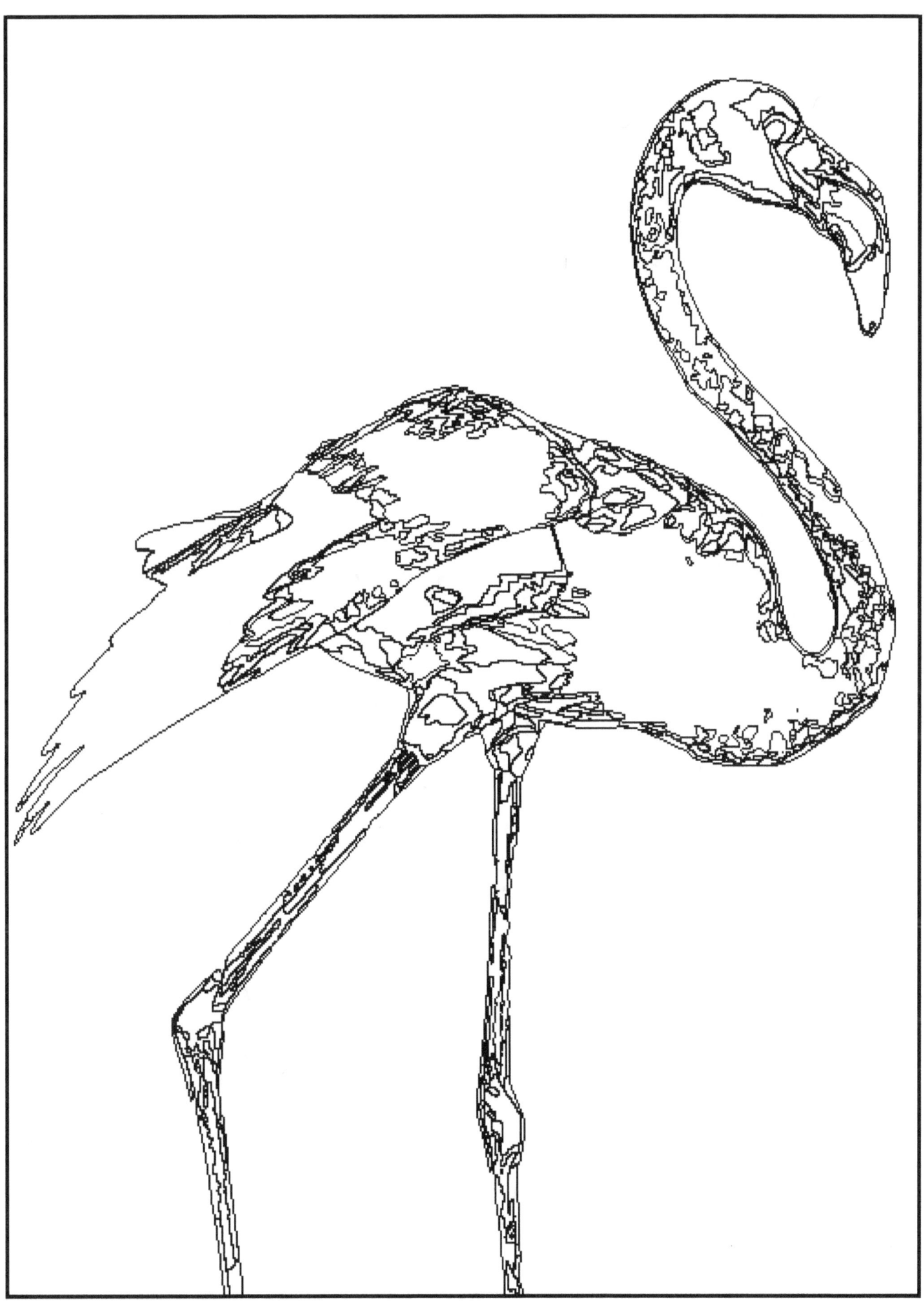

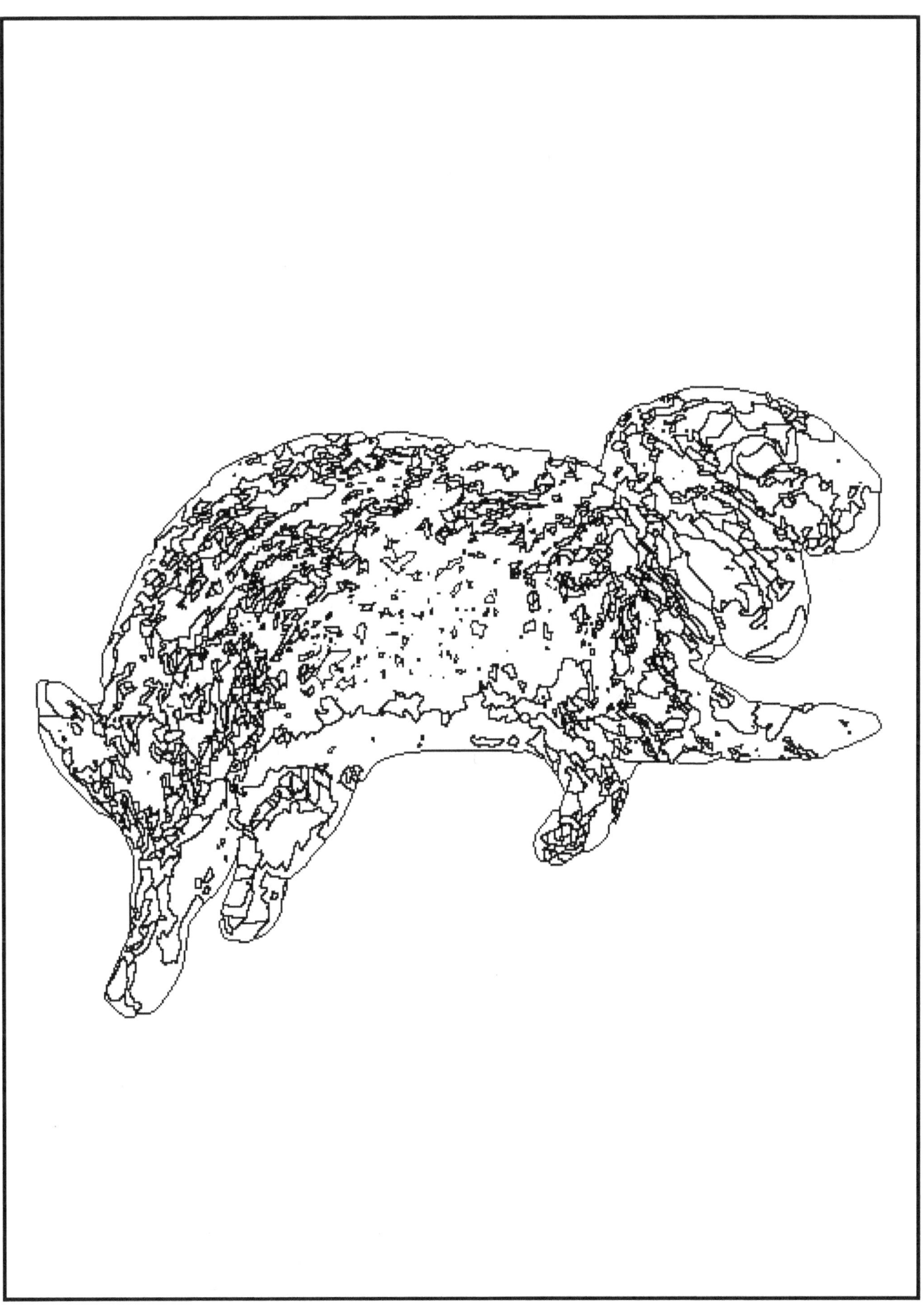

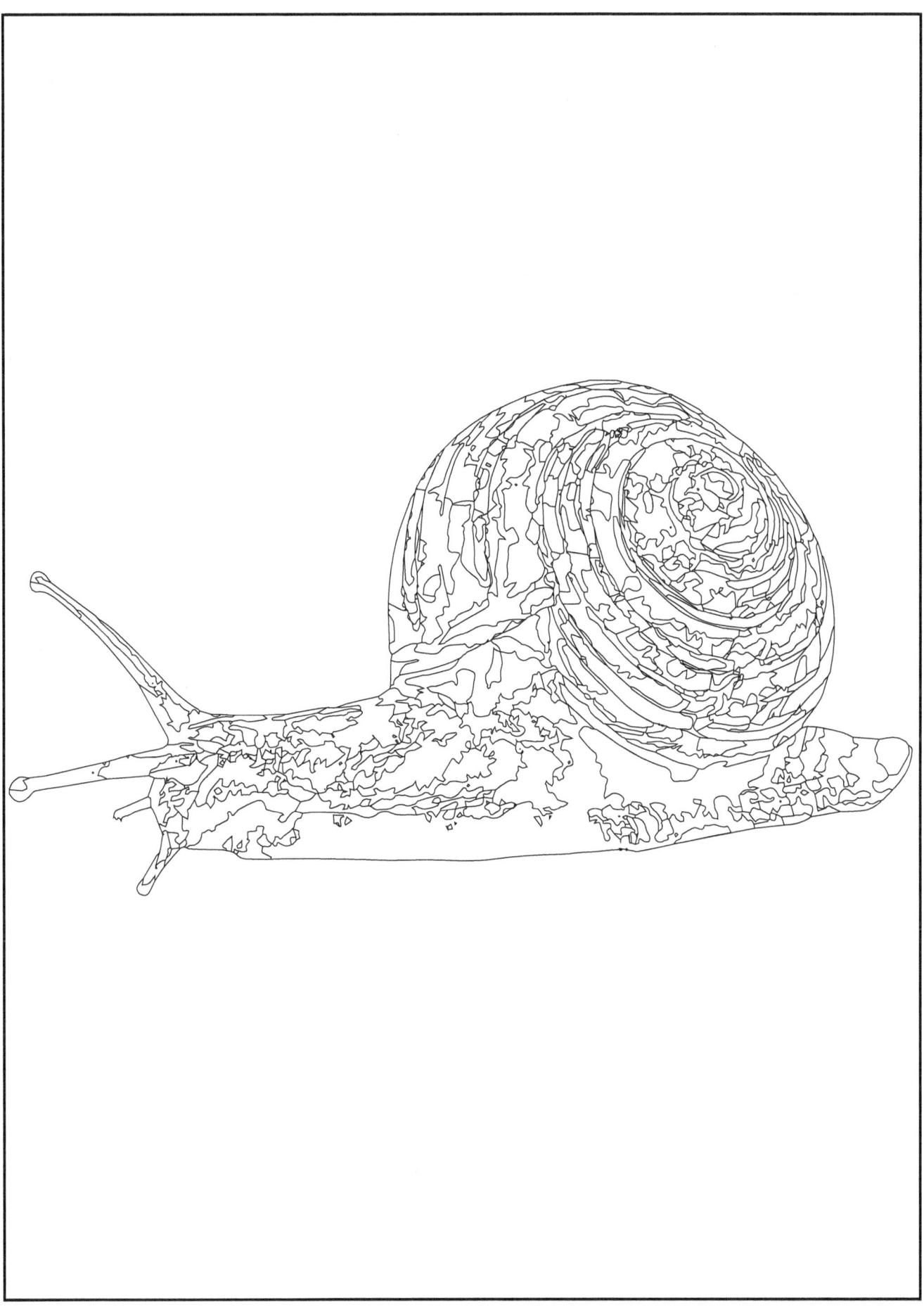

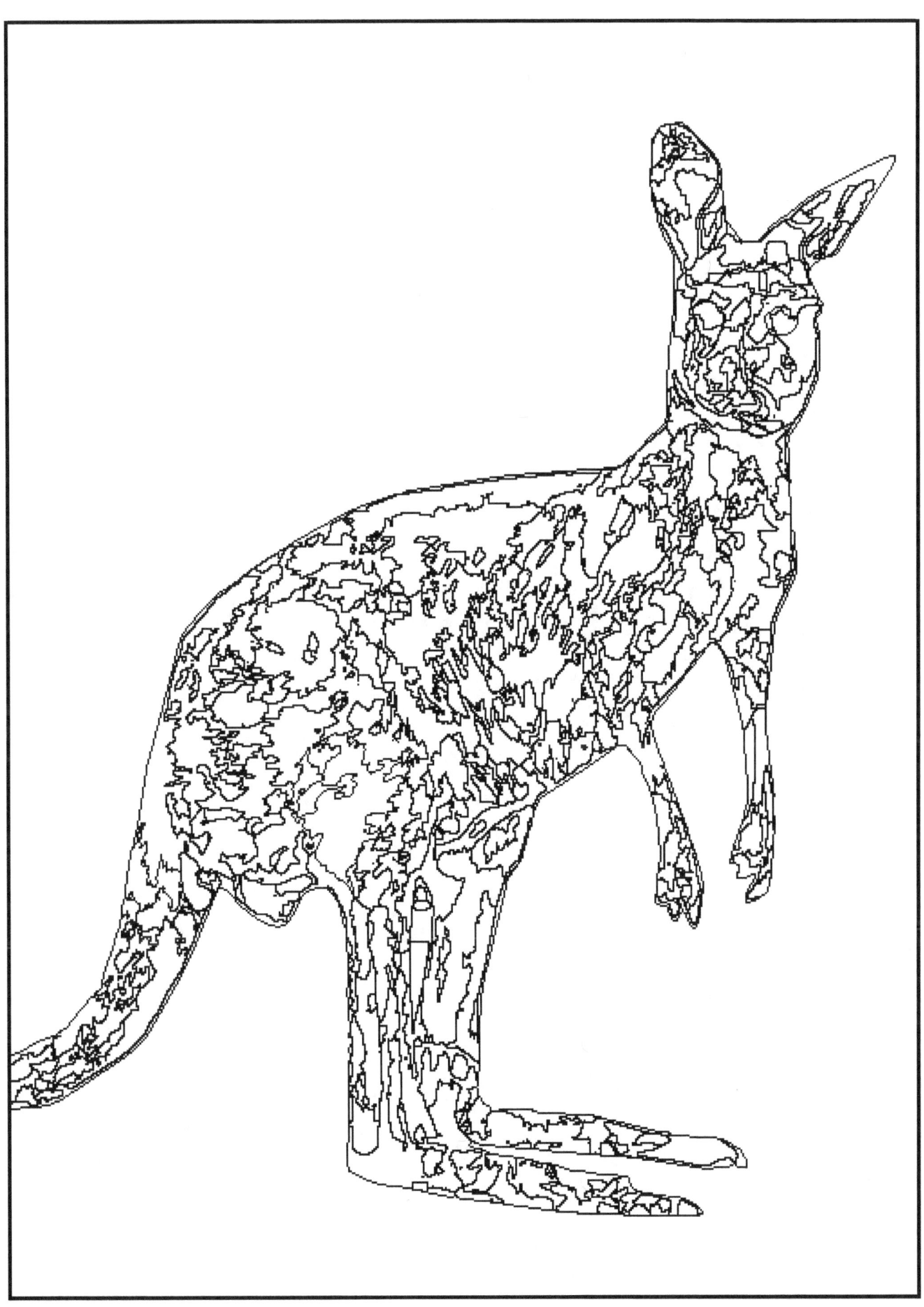

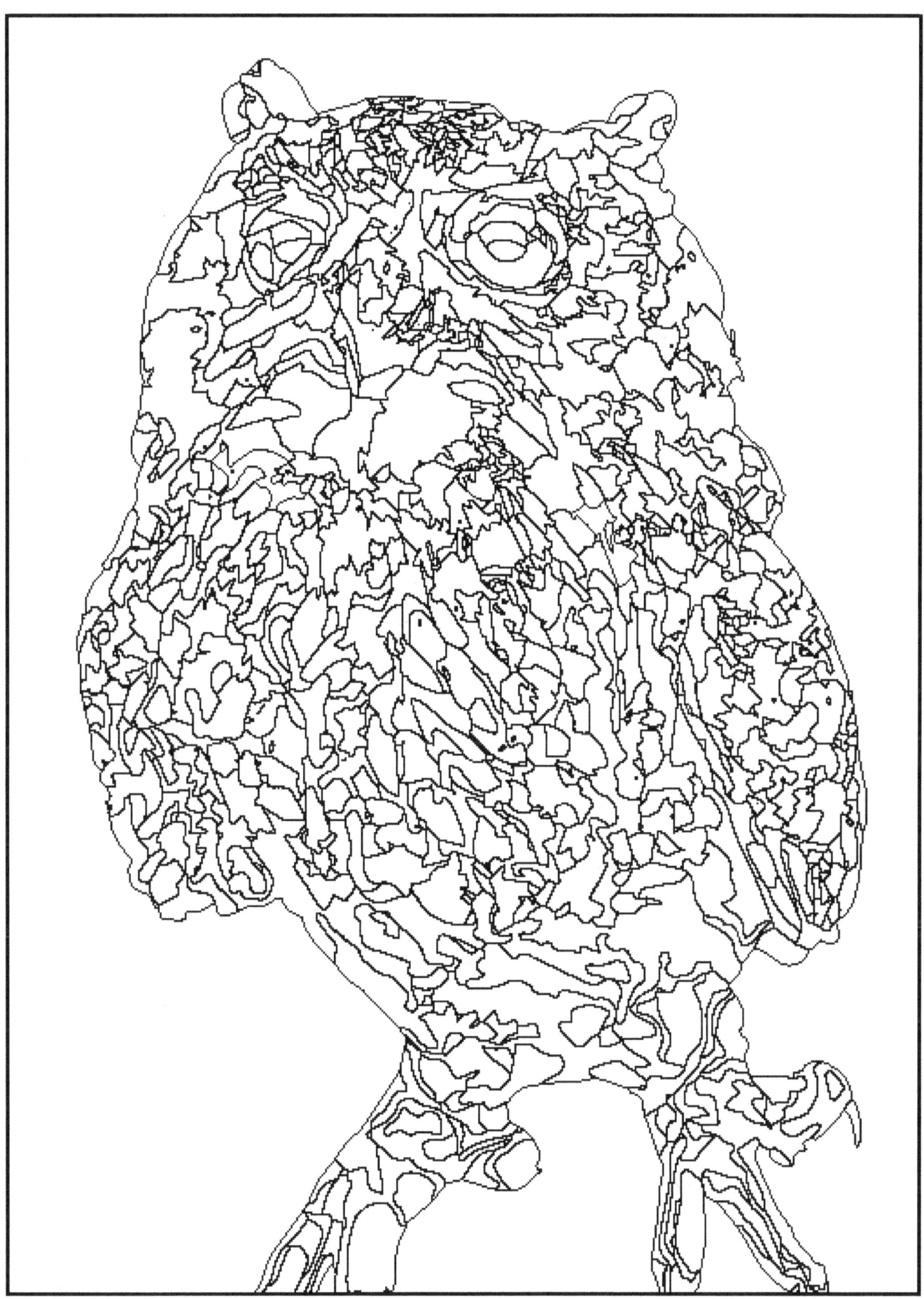

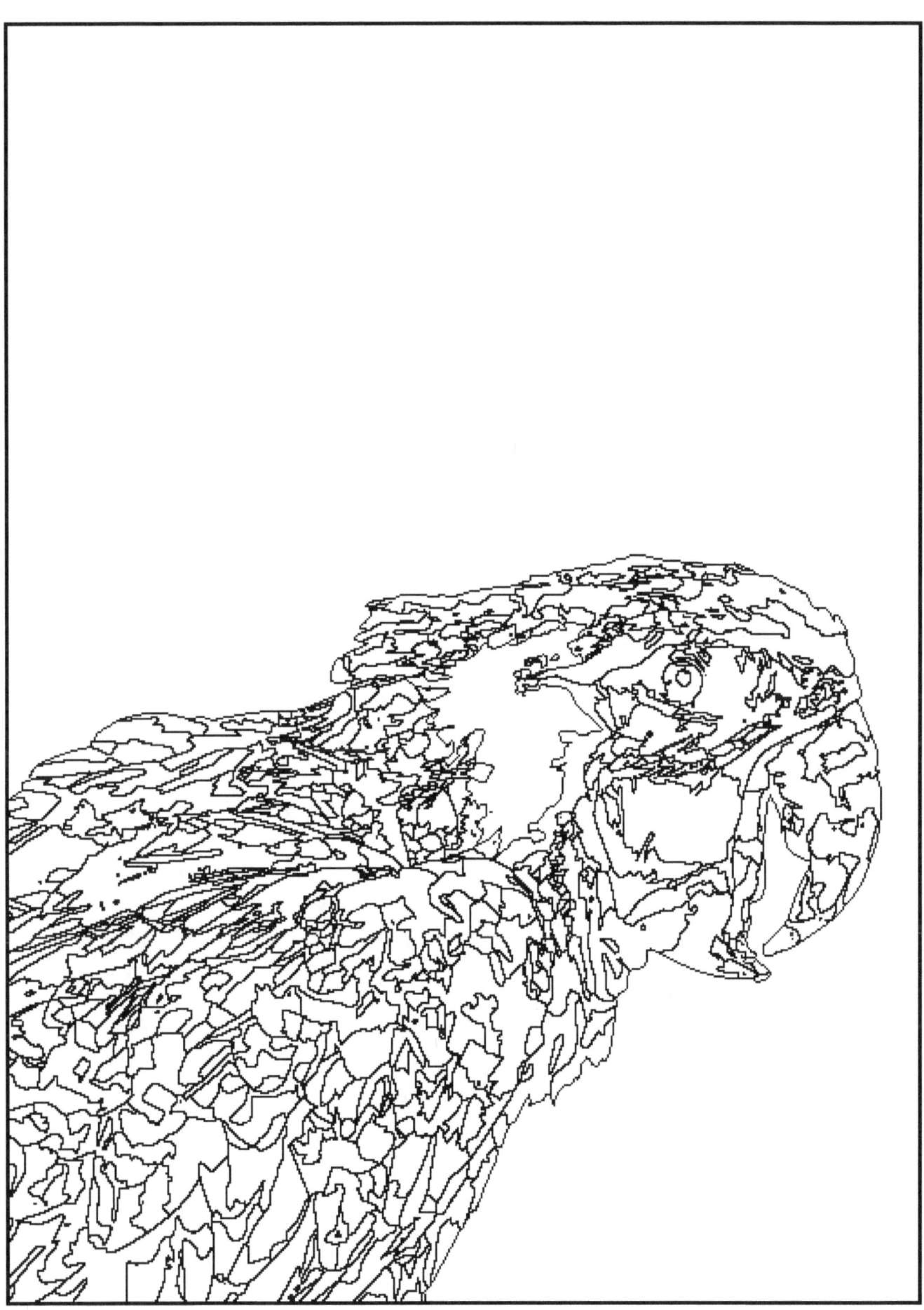

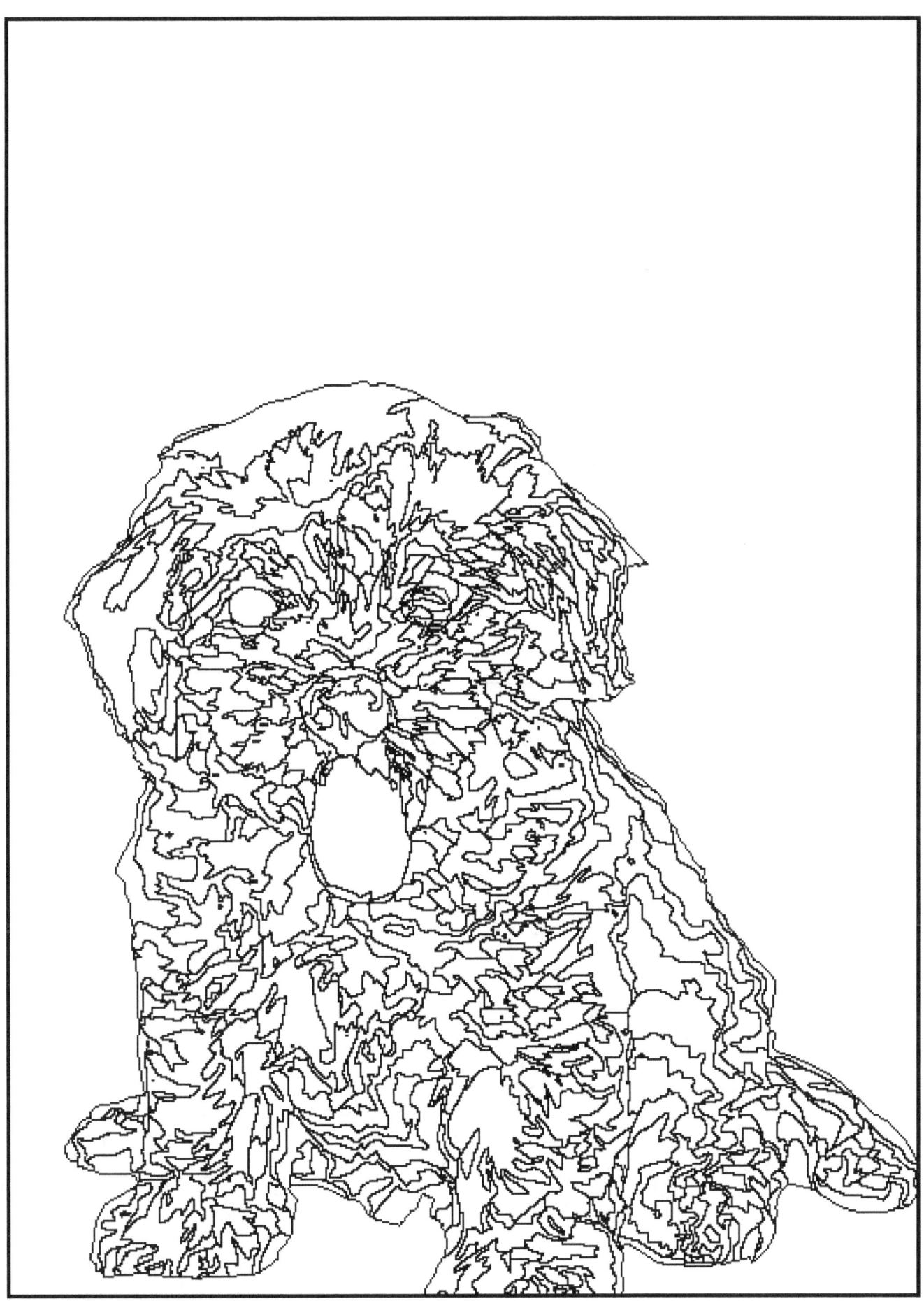

Congratulations on finishing!

If you get the chance, please consider leaving an honest review on Amazon! We appreciate each one.

www.ingramcontent.com/pod-product-compliance
Lightning Source LLC
Chambersburg PA
CBHW081057240526
45465CB00025B/2498